the
VINEYARDS
of
FRANCE

CHAMPAGNE

CHABLIS

POUILLY

CÔTE
DE BEAUNE

CÔTE
DE NUITS

ALSACE

CÔTES
DU
JURA

BURGUNDY

MÂCONNAIS

BEAUJOLAIS

CÔTES DU RHÔNE

rhône

CLAIRETTE
DE
DIE

MUSCATS

Pâté de campagne (Country pâté)

MARY REYNOLDS

FRENCH
cooking for pleasure

HAMLYN
LONDON · NEW YORK · SYDNEY · TORONTO

ILLUSTRATOR   Rosemary Aldridge
DESIGNER   Veronica Mathew

Published by
THE HAMLYN PUBLISHING GROUP LIMITED
LONDON · NEW YORK · SYDNEY · TORONTO
Hamlyn House, Feltham, Middlesex, England
© Copyright Mary Reynolds 1966
ISBN 0 600 01299 9
Fourth impression 1971
Printed in Czechoslovakia by PZ, Bratislava
52028

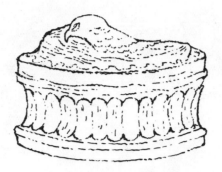

CONTENTS

INTRODUCTION

You don't need to remember a word of French to enjoy using this book. Neither will you need to waste time referring to glossaries of technical terms. All the recipes are given in plain English and methods have been described in detail without resort to chef-cum-haute-cuisine culinary jargon. For this is intended as a first book of French cooking for keen but busy people who love to cook.

My hope is that if you found a dish you enjoyed on holiday, or when dining out, you will find a recipe for it in this book and be able to reproduce it at home, complete with authentic aroma, flavour and appearance. The majority of recipes selected are typical of those served in ordinary French homes and family restaurants. A few more lavish dishes come from two star restaurants but in the main the recipes follow the modern French trend towards simpler food. Lack of domestic help, and the general speed of life are changing traditional standards in France as everywhere else.

French food and drink are strongly regional in character and from province to province. Many popular regional recipes have been included in this book but dishes for which it is difficult to find the right ingredients have been omitted — hence no bouillabaisse or crêpes de sarrasin.

So much has been written about fabulous French restaurants that you may be surprised at the simplicity and economy of many of the recipes. But the truth is that by tradition French women are extremely practical housekeepers and not given to extravagance. Good food is expensive, and in a French home it is never wasted. Anything left over from one meal will be served, possibly in disguise, at the next. Haricot verts from one meal for instance will appear in a Salade Niçoise at the next. Food in season, and hence at its cheapest and best, will be served day after day as long as the season lasts.

'The secret of fine French food' said a famous gastronome, 'is primarily the careful selection of the ingredients' and this is much in evidence when you watch a French woman shopping. She uses her eyes, nose and fingers, as well as her head, to check quality and compare values before she buys. Having obtained the best possible raw materials the art of the French cook is then directed to bringing out their full flavour. And this is where a little patience and attention to detail in cooking really does pay dividends. If, for instance, the recipe says 'dry the meat or chicken joints thoroughly before frying', it is important to do so for this aids the browning process and seals in the juices in the meat. It takes a little time but it achieves a purpose. Often a recipe will direct you to 'reduce the liquid to half by rapid boiling' which is another typically French method of concentrating flavour and one that can make all the difference between a fine dish and a mediocre one. 'Simmer' really does mean simmer — that is to say cooking just below boiling point so that only an occasional bubble breaks the surface of the liquid. There can be no compromise with time either; if a recipe says 'simmer for 4 hours' the flavour will be infinitely better after 4 hours cooking than after 3, for only long slow cooking can achieve the right amalgamation of flavours to give the dish its character. This is especially so with French casserole dishes such as daubes, cassoulets and so on. Finally the author would like to express her gratitude to the many friends in France as well as England who have helped in various ways with the preparation of this book. And in particular to Françoise Bernard the well known French writer and broadcaster for her help in supplying certain pictures and information.

6

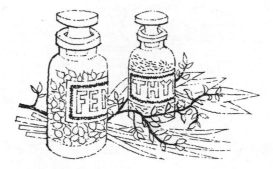

EATING THE FRENCH WAY

Good food is really important to the French. The moment of perfect ripeness of a pear, the relative merits of Normandy mussels or Bordeaux oysters, the quality of an olive, all are subjects for earnest discussion. And meal times are family occasions to be lingered over and enjoyed.

Inevitably French meals are as varied in style and quality as those of any other country but they follow a general pattern which is quite different from our own. Breakfast is scant, (hot coffee with roll and butter and possibly a croissant), mid-morning coffee and afternoon tea are rare events. The French housewife concentrates her time and effort on two main meals, one at mid-day and another in the evening.

Perhaps the most noticeable difference about these meals is the absence of 'meat and two veg' served together on one overcrowded plate. Instead several dishes are served one after the other as individual courses. The advantage of this system is that you really taste and appreciate the flavour and texture of each dish. Perhaps this is why French women cook with such loving care — they know their efforts will be savoured and enjoyed, and not merely consumed without comment.

A mid-day family meal might start with a sliced tomato salad, to be followed by an egg mayonnaise, a sauté of chicken or rabbit with potatoes, then a dish of vegetables, then cheese, followed by fresh fruit, tarte or gâteau, and finally black coffee. A red or white 'vin ordinaire' and a mineral water would be drunk with the meal, unless it was an 'occasion' when a wine or wines from a particular district or vineyard would be chosen. Two glasses are set for each place, one for wine and one for water. And of course crusty bread would be available right through the meal. Plates are changed between courses as necessary, but the practical French reduce washing up by setting a knife rest known as a 'portecouteau' beside each place on which knives and forks are 'rested' between courses. Fresh cutlery is used for the cheese and dessert.

Cheese is always served *before* the sweet or fruit in France, and wine served with the main course is finished with the cheese. Gravies consist of the meat juices to which a little butter or wine may be added but no thickening. Even in the best circles it is accepted that a good sauce or 'jus' deserves to be mopped up with bread rather than wasted. Green salads tossed in oil and vinegar dressing at the very last minute are served frequently, after or with the main course.

If the main meal of the day is taken at mid-day the evening meal will be simpler and lighter. Invariably it will begin with soup followed by an egg dish such as an omelette or eggs en cocotte, or perhaps a gratin dish or a savoury tart; cheese or a salad followed by fruit would complete the meal.

Rich food does not figure in French homes nearly as frequently as one might suppose, for one thing the cost is prohibitive and for another the French are quite as diet and health conscious as the rest of us. What most typifies good French cooking is high quality raw materials cooked simply but perfectly to enhance their natural flavour.

WEIGHTS AND MEASURES

Weights throughout the book are given in lb. and oz. Capacity measure is given in Imperial pints and fractions thereof, with small amounts in spoon measures. For the benefit of American readers liquid ingredients have been given to the nearest U.S. standard cup measure. These follow the English measure i.e. 1 pint (U.S. 2½ cups). All spoon measures refer to the British Standards Institution. All measures are levelled off to the rim of the spoon. To measure fractions of spoons use the small measures provided in the sets of measuring spoons or divide the level spoon. The American standard measuring spoons are slightly smaller in capacity than the British standard measuring spoons. The proportion however is similar in that 3 American standard teaspoons equal 1 tablespoon.

HANDY CONVERSION TABLE
(Approximate conversion table)

ENGLISH MEASURE		AMERICAN MEASURE
1 lb.	Butter or other fat	2 cups
1 lb.	Flour (sifted)	4 cups
1 lb.	Granulated or Castor Sugar	2¼ cups
1 lb.	Icing or Confectioners' Sugar	3½ cups
1 lb.	Brown (moist) Sugar	2¼ cups
1 lb.	Golden Syrup or Treacle	1⅓ cup
1 lb.	Rice	2¼—2½ cups
1 lb.	Dried Fruit (chopped)	2—2½ cups
1 lb.	Raw Chopped Meat (finely packed)	2 cups
1 lb.	Lentils or Split Peas	2 cups
1 lb.	Coffee (unground)	2½ cups
1 lb.	Dry Breadcrumbs	4 cups
8 oz.	Butter or Margarine	1 cup
8 oz.	Lard	1 cup
7 oz.	Castor Sugar	1 cup
7 oz.	Soft Brown Sugar	1 cup (packed)
7 oz.	Candied Fruit	1 cup
6⅓ oz.	Chopped Dates	1 cup
6 oz.	Chocolate Pieces	1 cup
5 oz.	Currants	1 cup
5½ oz.	Cooked Rice	1 cup
5¾ oz.	Seedless Raisins	1 cup

5 oz.	Candied Peel	1 cup
5 oz.	Chopped Mixed Nuts	1 cup
5 oz.	Sliced Apple	1 cup
4½ oz.	Icing Sugar	1 cup (sifted)
4 oz.	Cheddar Cheese	1 cup (grated)
3½ oz.	Cocoa	1 cup
2½ oz.	Desiccated Coconut	1 cup
2 oz.	Fresh breadcrumbs	1 cup
1 oz.	Plain Dessert Chocolate	1 square
¼ oz.	Dried Yeast	1 packet
¼ oz.	Gelatine	1 tablespoon
¾ tablespoon	Gelatine	1 envelope
½ oz.	Flour	1 level tablespoon*
1 oz.	Flour	2 level tablespoons
1 oz.	Sugar	1 level tablespoon
½ oz.	Butter	1 level tablespoon smoothed off
1 oz.	Golden Syrup or Treacle	1 level tablespoon
1 oz.	Jam or Jelly	1 level tablespoon

* must be standard U.S. measuring tablespoon

METRIC EQUIVALENTS

It is rather difficult to convert from English to French measures with absolute accuracy, but 1 oz. is equal to approximately 30 grammes, 2 lb. 3 oz. is equal to 1 kilogramme. For liquid measure, approximately 1¾ English pints may be regarded as equal to 1 litre; ½ pint is equal to 3 decilitres (scant); 3½ fluid oz. is equal to 1 decilitre.

OVEN TEMPERATURES

DESCRIPTION OF OVEN	Approximate temperature centre of oven °F	THERMOSTAT SETTING
Very slow or	200—250	¼ = 240
Very cool		½ = 265
		1 = 290
Slow or Cool	250—300	2 = 310
Very Moderate	300—350	3 = 335
Moderate	350—375	4 = 350
Moderately Hot		5 = 375
to Hot	375—400	6 = 400
Hot to Very Hot	425—450	7 = 425
Very hot	450—500	8 = 450
		9 = 470

Note

THIS TABLE IS AN APPROXIMATE GUIDE ONLY. DIFFERENT MAKES OF COOKER VARY AND IF YOU ARE IN ANY DOUBT ABOUT THE SETTING IT IS AS WELL TO REFER TO THE MANUFACTURER'S TEMPERATURE CHART.

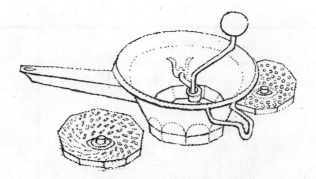

KITCHEN EQUIPMENT

The right tools make the cook's work easier and pleasanter. The items listed below are used over and over again in this book as well as the usual assortment of utensils and pans, including a double saucepan, and a deep roasting tin for use as a bain-marie.

1 An 8-inch fluted flan ring with false bottom.

2 Small wire whisk for sauces and mixing generally.

3 An 8-inch plain flan ring for savoury tarts.

4 Straight sided china soufflé dishes, in several sizes.

5 Heavy non-stick 10-inch frying pan, and a similar 6-inch pan for omelettes and pancakes.

6 Mandoline for shredding and slicing vegetables and cutting potato chips.

7 Oven proof gratin dishes in several sizes.

8 Enamelled cast iron casserole for use on top of the cooker as well as in the oven. In several shapes and sizes for preference.

9 Small pestle and mortar for grinding and pounding jobs, although many of these can now be done in an electric liquidiser.

10 Shallow 6-inch enamelled cast iron dish for cooking and serving eggs in the same dish.

11 Shallow oven proof dishes in several different sizes.

12 An earthenware terrine with lid for pâtés.

13 Large oval enamelled cast iron casserole known in France as a 'fait-tout'. Used on top of the cooker and in the oven for 'chicken en cocotte', daubes, and many slow cooking dishes.

14 A 9 — 10-inch sauté pan (shallow straight sided pan for sautéing meat or poultry). Particularly useful if it has a lid for food that has first to be browned and then covered to finish cooking.

15 Individual china or earthenware cocottes. Used for egg dishes, mousses and pâtés.

16 Pepper mill for grinding peppercorns freshly.

17 Vegetable sieve known as a 'mouli-legume' for sieving soups and making purées.

18 Salt mill for grinding gros sel or sea salt.

19 Sturdy wooden chopping board.

20 Flat wooden spatula for stirring into the corners of pans.

21 Carbon steel French cooks knives which can be kept razor sharp on a butchers steel.

22 Parisian vegetable cutter for scooping out potato and melon 'balls'.

10

Kitchen Equipment

Artichokes à la Vinaigrette (Artichokes with vinaigrette)

HORS-D'OEUVRE

LES HORS-D'OEUVRES

Mid-day meals in France invariably begin with an interesting 'little' first course designed to whet the appetite and stimulate the gastric juices. In the home this is usually a simple affair consisting of a single dish such as a savoury open tart, a pâté, a salad or a perfectly cooked vegetable. Or it may be a few assorted ingredients attractively arranged — ham or garlic sausage perhaps, or tunny fish, with black olives, red radishes and sliced tomatoes dressed with a herb vinaigrette. Crisp French bread and creamy butter will be on the table too, and usually a dry white wine. The important point about an hors-d'oeuvre is that all the ingredients should be fresh and of excellent quality — in short appetising. And the arrangement should be attractive but simple — *good* French food is seldom messy or over garnished. White or white lined dishes are excellent for presenting an hors-d'œuvre for they enhance the colours of the food where a patterned dish is liable to dull and confuse them. The perennial question 'what on earth can we start with' need be a problem no longer. In this chapter you will find an enormous variety of ideas — for fish, meat, vegetable and salad dishes . . .

HORS-D'OEUVRE VARIÉ
MIXED HORS-D'OEUVRE

To be good a mixed hors-d'oeuvre should be composed of different textures as well as a variety of flavours. Although for formal meals or a buffet the ingredients are usually set out in separate dishes, for a family meal it is simpler to arrange them attractively on individual plates. Try to include *one or more* items from each of the following.

SOMETHING CRISP AND RAW: radishes, strips of celery, fennel root dressed with vinaigrette à la crème (see page 109), thinly sliced red or green pepper, grated raw carrot, sliced tomatoes or cucumber.

MEAT OR FISH: a slice of salami, ham, garlic sausage, pâté or jellied pork. Canned sardines or tunny fish, cold cooked mackerel or herring fillets, shellfish.

SOMETHING SALT: anchovies in oil, or olives.

SOMETHING SOFT: a cooked vegetable salad dressed with mayonnaise (see page 119).

HORS-D'OEUVRE IDEAS FROM
OTHER CHAPTERS

PÂTÉS: any of the pâté recipes beginning page 28. Serve from the terrine or turned out and sliced, with hot toast or French bread and creamy butter.

SAVOURY PASTRIES: Quiche Lorraine, onion tart, bouchées or any of the recipes in the chapter beginning page 125.

SALADS: Salad Niçoise is the classic hors-d'oeuvre of the Mediterranean. Salade de Tomates. Salade Cauchoise, or any of the mixed salads in chapter (on page 108) make attractive meal starters.

EGGS: Oeufs en cocotte, omelette or any of the egg dishes in chapter 39.

VEGETABLES: Any young tender and perfectly cooked vegetable makes an excellent meal starter. May be cold, such as Ratatouille (page 98) or Poireaux à la Niçoise (page 104) or hot, such as Haricots Verts à la Provençale (page 98) or Aubergine aux Tomates (page 104). See Vegetable chapter page 97.

13

ARTICHOKES A LA VINAIGRETTE

ARTICHOKES WITH VINAIGRETTE

Preparation time 5 minutes
Cooking time 25–35 minutes
To serve 1

You will need

1 large fresh globe artichoke per person
salt
vinegar or lemon juice
vinaigrette with herbs (see page 109)

Choose compact and heavy artichokes. Trim the stem and base so that the artichoke will stand upright when served. Rinse in cold water and shake. Drop into a deep pan of boiling salted water acidulated with vinegar or lemon juice (1 tablespoon per 2 pints) and boil gently, uncovered, for 25–35 minutes. When cooked the leaves will pull out easily and the base is tender. Remove and drain *upside down* in a colander. Serve *cold*, on individual dessert size plates with a small cocotte of vinaigrette alongside. To eat, pull the leaves off individually and dip the fleshy end into the dressing before eating; discard the rest of the leaf. When the centre of the artichoke is reached cut off the fibrous 'choke'. The delicate base, known as the 'fond artichoke' is then cut up and eaten with knife and fork. Finger bowls should be provided.

Miniature fish balls

VARIATION
ARTICHOKES AU BEURRE FONDU
ARTICHOKES WITH MELTED BUTTER

Cook the artichokes as above but serve with *warm* melted butter to which a few drops of lemon juice have been added.

SALADE DE MOULES PROVENÇALES

MUSSEL SALAD PROVENÇAL STYLE

(Illustrated in colour on page 19)

Scrape and scrub 4 pints (U.S. 10 cups) mussels clean; wash in several lots cold water. Discard any mussels which do not close tightly when tapped. Heat 2 tablespoons olive oil and fry 4 oz. finely chopped onion over low heat. Add 1 lb. ripe tomatoes, and a crushed clove of garlic and cook for 5 minutes. Add mussels, cover and cook over brisk heat, shaking frequently, until shells open, about 5–6 minutes. Remove, discard shells and put mussels in a shallow dish. Boil tomato sauce rapidly until reduced to a thin sauce consistency; season with ground black pepper and sieve. Spoon over mussels.

BEIGNETS DE POISSON

MINIATURE FISH BALLS

Any cooked white fish can be used but these fish balls are particularly delicious made with smoked haddock. Mash 8 oz. freshly boiled potato with 1 oz. butter. Add 12 oz. cooked flaked fish free from all skin and bone; 2 oz. onion, finely chopped and fried soft but not brown; 1 beaten egg and seasoning to taste. Mix very well and form into walnut size balls. Coat thoroughly with flour and leave until firm. Fry in hot oil or fat (all ingredients are cooked so frying can be quick) then drain on kitchen paper. Serve hot with melted butter or cream sauce handed separately.

CHAMPIGNONS A LA GRECQUE

MUSHROOMS STEWED IN OIL AND WINE

(Also illustrated in colour on the jacket)
Preparation time 5 minutes
Cooking time   10–12 minutes
To serve   2–4 (depending if other dishes served)

You will need

4 tablespoons olive oil
4 tablespoons water
2 tablespoons white wine
1 tablespoon lemon juice
1 level tablespoon chopped onion
1 level teaspoon tomato purée
½ bay leaf
salt and ground black pepper
8 oz. small button mushrooms

Put all ingredients except the button mushrooms into a pan and allow to simmer for 5 minutes. Wash the button mushrooms (if large cut into halves or quarters) and add to the ingredients in the pan. Simmer for 6—8 minutes, stirring occasionally. Drain the mushrooms and arrange in a shallow dish. Reduce liquid to a syrupy consistency by boiling rapidly for a minute or two, then pour over the mushrooms.
Serve cold, alone, or in a mixed hors-d'oeuvre.

Mushrooms stewed in oil and wine

PETITS OIGNONS AUX RAISINS

BUTTON ONIONS WITH RAISINS

(Illustrated in colour on the jacket)
Preparation time 15 minutes
Cooking time   1½ hours
To serve   2–4

You will need

1½ oz. butter
1 tablespoon olive oil
1 lb. button onions, peeled
3 oz. seedless raisins *or* sultanas
sprig each thyme and parsley
small bay leaf
salt and pepper
½ pint (U. S. 1¼ cups) dry white wine

Melt the butter and oil in a flameproof casserole or strong saucepan. Add the onions and cook over a low heat for about 10 minutes, until a light golden brown, shaking the pan frequently. Drain off the fat. Add the raisins *or* sultanas, thyme, parsley, bay leaf, seasoning and wine. Cover closely and simmer *very gently* for 1 hour. Using a perforated spoon transfer the onions and raisins to a shallow serving dish (or individual dishes) and discard the herbs. Reduce the wine to a syrupy consistency by rapid boiling, then pour over the onions.
Serve cold, alone, or in a mixed hors-d'oeuvre.

ANCHOIADE
PROVENÇALE ANCHOVY TOASTS

Pre-heat an oven to hot (425°F. or Gas Mark 7). Mash 2 cloves garlic and contents of a 4 oz. can anchovy fillets to a paste. Gradually add 1 tablespoon olive oil and 3—4 drops wine vinegar. Toast 8 thick slices French bread on one side only; cover *untoasted* side with anchovy paste; press well in. Heat near the top of the oven for 4—5 minutes. Serve hot.

Hard-boiled eggs Toulon style

OEUFS A LA TOULONNAISE

HARD-BOILED EGGS TOULON STYLE

Preparation time 15 minutes
Cooking time no cooking
To serve 3 (more if part of a mixed hors-d'oeuvre)

You will need

3 hard-boiled eggs
2 oz. anchovy fillets
¼ pint thick mayonnaise (see page 119)

Cut the hard-boiled eggs in half lengthwise and arrange cut side down in a shallow dish. Cut the anchovy fillets into thin strips. If necessary thin the mayonnaise to a thick coating consistency with creamy milk, then coat the eggs. Band each egg with anchovy strips as in the picture. Serve alone, or as part of a mixed hors-d'oeuvre.

CAROTTES RAPÉES

GRATED CARROT SALAD

A popular ingredient for a mixed hors-d'oeuvre. Scrape 1 lb. young carrots and shred on a coarse grater. Add 1 tablespoon finely chopped shallot *or* onion, 2—3 tablespoons olive oil, 1 dessertspoon of lemon juice and salt to taste. Serve sprinkled with chopped parsley *or* chives.

CRÈME DE THON A LA MIRABEAU

TUNNY FISH CREAMS

Preparation time 10–15 minutes
Cooking time no cooking
To serve 4

You will need

6 oz. can tunny fish
3 oz. unsalted butter, softened
1–2 tablespoons olive oil
ground black pepper
1–2 teaspoons lemon juice
12 black olives, halved and stoned
4 firm tomatoes, sliced

Pound the tunny fish to a paste then work in the butter. Beat in sufficient oil to give a creamy texture. Season to taste with pepper and lemon juice (or blend all ingredients together at medium speed in an electric blender). Divide, and shape each portion into a mound in 4 individual gratin dishes. Stud the surface with halved olives and circle the base with halved tomato slices. Hand hot toast fingers separately.

MAQUEREAUX AU VIN BLANC

MACKEREL IN WHITE WINE

Preparation time 15 minutes
Cooking time 20 minutes
To serve 4

4 small mackerel
½ oz. butter *or* margarine
1 small carrot, thinly sliced
2 small onions, thinly sliced
2 slices lemon
salt and ground black pepper
½ pint (U.S. 1¼ cups) dry white wine
1 tablespoon chopped herbs (parsley, chervil and chives)

Clean and wash the mackerel. Grease a shallow ovenproof dish and strew the carrot, onions and lemon over the bottom. Arrange the fish on top. Sprinkle with salt and pepper and pour the wine over. Scatter the herbs on top. Cook in a moderate oven (375°F. or Gas Mark 5), for 20 minutes, basting once or twice. Leave to cool in the liquid, and, when cold serve in the same dish.

Note

For a more elegant dish the mackerel are sometimes skinned and filleted then covered with the strained and reduced cooking liquor. Fresh herring may be cooked in the same way.

ESCARGOTS A LA BOURGUIGNONNE

STUFFED SNAILS BURGUNDY STYLE

Preparation time 15 minutes
Cooking time   10 minutes
To serve   1

You will need

Beurre d'Escargots (Garlic Butter, see page 118)
1 dozen canned snails
1 dozen snail shells
indented snail dish

The preparation of snails is a long and tedious job so most people nowadays buy canned snails which have been specially reared for the table. Empty shells bought separately can be washed and

Mackerel in white wine

used again. Prepare the garlic and parsley flavoured butter. Put a little piece into each shell, slip in the snail, and pack firmly to the brim with more butter. Place shells, open end up, in snail dishes, cover with greased foil and cook in a pre-heated moderately hot oven (400°F. or Gas Mark 6), for about 10 minutes. Serve at once, keeping dishes upright to retain the butter in the shells. In restaurants pincers are provided for holding the shell while the snail is extracted with a forked pick.

LES TOMATES A LA PARISIENNE

STUFFED TOMATOES PARIS STYLE

(Illustrated in colour on page 19)

Cut a slice off stem end of 8 tomatoes, scoop out pulp. Sprinkle cavity with salt; leave upside down to drain. Chop 6 oz. white crabmeat, lobster, crawfish, prawns *or* shrimps roughly and mix with 3 tablespoons thick mayonnaise (see page 119). Fill tomato cases and replace lids. Serve cold.

LES HUITRES

OYSTERS

(Illustrated in colour on page 114)

Oysters are a favourite hors-d'oeuvre in France. When serving raw allow 6 to 12 very fresh oysters per serving, depending on size. Always keep the deep shell underneath so that the liquid is retained, and unless expert with an oyster knife ask the fishmonger to open them for you. Serve with lemon slices, fresh bread and butter and a dry white wine such as a Chablis *or* Muscadet.

TOMATES ACCORDÉON

ACCORDION TOMATOES

Wipe 4 tomatoes and place stem down on a board. Slice downwards almost to the base but without cutting through. Slice 4 hard-boiled eggs thinly roundwise. Open out each tomato like a concertina and slip a slice of egg between each tomato slice. Arrange on individual dishes and spoon a dessertspoon thick mayonnaise (see page 119) over each. Sprinkle with chopped parsley *or* chives.

CÉLERI-RAVE RÉMOULADE

CELERIAC WITH
MUSTARD MAYONNAISE

(Illustrated in colour on the jacket)
Preparation time 15–20 minutes
Cooking time 3 minutes
To serve 3–6 (depending on other
 ingredients served)

You will need

1 celeriac (12–16 oz.)
little lemon juice
salt
¼ pint (U.S. ⅝ cup) mayonnaise (see page 119)
1 tablespoon chopped parsley

Wash the celeriac and peel coarsely. Cut into thin slices then into match sticks about 1-inch long (a mandoline, see page 10, makes short work of this), and immediately drop into cold water acidulated with lemon juice. Drain, plunge into boiling water and cook for 2 minutes only; drain and cool. Meanwhile prepare mayonnaise adding 2—3 times the usual quantity of mustard to give a strong mustard flavour. Mix the cold celeriac and mayonnaise lightly together. Pile into a dish and sprinkle with parsley. Serve soon after preparing, alone, or as part of a mixed hors-d'oeuvre.

SARDINES AUX OEUFS
DURS ET CITRON

SARDINES WITH HARD-BOILED
EGGS AND LEMON

(Illustrated in colour opposite)
Preparation time 15 minutes
Cooking time no cooking
To serve 2–4

You will need

8 large sardines in oil
2 hard-boiled eggs
1 lemon, thinly sliced
sprigs parsley

A simple family first course or part of a mixed hors-d'oeuvre.
Arrange the sardines neatly to suit the shape of the dish — head to tail or in a circle or fan shape. Chop the egg white and press the yolk through a coarse sieve; arrange in a heap in the centre of the sardines. Garnish the dish with lemon slices and sprigs of parsley. This practical hors-d'oeuvre is quickly put together from store cupboard ingredients, yet is typical French family fare. Use only the best quality sardines in oil.

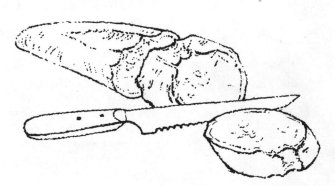

Hors-d'oeuvre varié (Mixed hors-d'oeuvre)

Soupe de poisson (Fish soup)

SOUPS

LES POTAGES

Soup has always been one of the mainstays of French home cooking. Although luncheon usually begins with an hors-d'oeuvre, soup invariably introduces the evening meal. Perhaps a consommé or delicate cream soup to start a formal meal, but often a hearty country soup followed by salad, cheese and crusty bread *is* the meal. Many French soups start with water as the liquid ingredient, but where stock is specified commercial stock cubes are excellent provided you remember these are highly seasoned. If fresh stock from boiling a piece of beef or carcase of a chicken or turkey happens to be handy you would of course use this. The vegetable

and cream of vegetable soups are delicious. This is because in the initial stages the cut up vegetables are thoroughly mixed with butter and then 'sweated' gently over a low heat before any liquid is added. Another French trick, stirring in a little fresh cream or butter just before serving the soup is a wonderful way of enriching the flavour.

Although the suggested number of servings is given for each recipe, please use your discretion — appetites vary enormously and much depends whether the soup is a starter or the mainstay of a meal. Even if the former, plates often come for second helpings . . .

SERVING FRENCH SOUPS

Crusty French bread, crisped and warmed in the oven for a few minutes if you like, and fresh creamy butter are essential companions for good soups. A sprinkling of chopped fresh herbs is always pleasing and the crunch of buttery croûtons in contrast to a purée or cream soup well worth the few minutes needed to make them.

CROÛTONS

Cut $\frac{1}{4}$-inch cubes of firm bread and fry slowly in hot butter and oil until golden and crisp. Drain well.

CROÛTES

Croûtes are handed with vegetable and fish soups. Slice $\frac{1}{4}$-inch thick slices of French bread on the slant. Bake in a slow oven until dry and pale brown, about 30 minutes. For fish soups the croûtes are rubbed with garlic and sprinkled with olive oil before baking.

SOUPE A L'OSEILLE
SORREL SOUP

Preparation time 15 minutes
Cooking time   1 hour
To serve   4

You will need

4 oz. fresh sorrel, washed and cut into fine shreds
1 oz. butter
8 oz. potatoes, peeled and diced
1½ pints (U.S. 3¾ cups) water
salt and pepper to taste
1 egg yolk
2 tablespoons milk
croûtons (see opposite), to serve separately

Melt butter in pan, add sorrel and cook over low heat until soft. Add potatoes, water and seasoning; bring to the boil. Cover; simmer for 1 hour. Sieve and reheat. Beat egg yolk and milk together in a warm tureen and stir in the boiling soup.

21

Toasted onion soup

SOUPE A L'OIGNON

ONION SOUP

Preparation time 15 minutes
Cooking time   about 30 minutes
To serve   4

You will need

1½ oz. butter
1 tablespoon oil
1 lb. Spanish onions, thinly sliced
2 level teaspoons sugar
2 pints (U.S. 5 cups) boiling beef stock
salt and pepper to season
4 or more bread croûtes (see page 21)
grated Gruyère *or* Parmesan cheese

This soup has the reputation of being a good pick-me-up. Heat the butter and oil in a heavy pan, add the onions and stir. Cover and cook over *low* heat until soft, 10—12 minutes. Sprinkle with the sugar and stir over moderate heat until pale gold. Add the stock and seasonings to taste. Cover, and simmer gently for 20—30 minutes. Put the bread croûtes into a tureen or individual earthenware bowls and pour the boiling soup over. Hand the cheese separately.

VARIATION
SOUPE À L'OIGNON GRATINÉE
TOASTED ONION SOUP

Sprinkle the bread croûtes with olive oil and then liberally with grated Gruyère cheese. Put into a flameproof tureen. Pour the boiling soup over, sprinkle with more cheese and slip under the

grill until bubbling and golden. Vary the amount of bread croûtes according to the thickness of soup required.

POTAGE JULIENNE AU BOUILLON

BOUILLON WITH VEGETABLES

Preparation time 20 minutes
Cooking time   20 minutes
To serve   4–6

You will need

2 leeks
2 medium-sized carrots   prepared and
1 medium-sized turnip   cut into match
1 medium-sized onion   size strips
4 oz. green cabbage (optional)
2 pints (U.S. 5 cups) bouillon from pot-au-feu
  or stock cube
salt and pepper
a little chopped fresh chervil *or* parsley

Put prepared vegetables into saucepan with 2 tablespoons of fat skimmed from bouillon, or if using a stock cube, butter. Cook over a low heat for 5 minutes, stirring occasionally. Add bouillon, cover and simmer for 15 minutes. Season if necessary and serve sprinkled with herbs.

POTAGE CRÉCY

PURÉE OF CARROT SOUP

Preparation time 15 minutes
Cooking time   30 minutes
To serve   4

You will need

1 lb. carrots, sliced
2 oz. butter
8 oz. potatoes, peeled and sliced
4 oz. onion, chopped
small sprig thyme, *or* ¼ teaspoon dried
1½ pints (U.S. 3¾ cups) white stock *or* water
salt, pepper and sugar to season
GARNISH
chopped fresh chervil *or* parsley
croûtons (see page 21)

Choose carrots of good red colour. Melt 1½ oz. butter in a heavy saucepan, add the carrots, potatoes, onion and thyme, and stir well.

Cover, and cook over *very low* heat, shaking the pan now and then, for 12—15 minutes. Add the liquid and seasonings. Cover, and simmer for about 20 minutes, until soft. Pass through a mouli, sieve or electric blender and return to the rinsed pan. Check seasoning and reheat. Just before serving stir in the remaining butter. Sprinkle with herbs and hand croûtons separately. Serve very hot.

CRÈME DE CRESSON

CREAM OF WATERCRESS SOUP

Preparation time 10 minutes
Cooking time 20 minutes
To serve 4

You will need

1 oz. butter
3 oz. onion, chopped
2 bunches watercress (6–8 oz.)
1 oz. plain flour
1½ pints (U.S. 3¾ cups) chicken stock
salt, pepper
2 egg yolks
4 tablespoons double cream

Cream of watercress soup

Melt butter in a thick saucepan, stir in onion, cover and cook over *low* heat until soft but not coloured. Meanwhile wash and inspect cress discarding all but fresh leaves and tender stalks. Dry, and reserve a few leaves for garnishing. Add cress to onion, stir and cook for a minute until wilted. Sprinkle in the flour, stir and cook for 2 minutes. Add stock and stir until boiling. Season to taste and simmer 5 minutes. Sieve soup, return to pan and reheat to simmering point. Mix egg yolks and cream in a basin, gradually stir in ½ pint of hot soup then return all to pan and reheat, stirring, *without boiling*. Float reserved leaves of cress on top and serve.

Note
This soup may also be served chilled.

CRÈME DE LAITUES

CREAM OF LETTUCE SOUP

Preparation time 10 minutes
Cooking time 40 minutes
To serve 4

You will need

2 large heads lettuce
2 oz. butter
4 oz. onion, sliced
1 pint (U.S. 2½ cups) chicken stock
½ pint (U.S. 1¼ cups) Béchamel Sauce
  (see page 120)
salt pepper and sugar to season
2 tablespoons double cream
  or ½ oz. butter
GARNISH
2 tablespoons chopped chervil *or* parsley
croûtons (see page 21)

An excellent use for surplus lettuce. Wash, dry and shred the lettuce leaves. Melt the butter in a large saucepan, add the onion and lettuce, stir, cover the pan and cook over *low* heat, stirring now and then, for 10—15 minutes. Add the stock, bring to the boil, cover, and simmer for 15 minutes. Sieve or purée the vegetables and return to the pan. Stir in the Béchamel Sauce and seasoning to taste. Reheat, and just before serving stir in the cream *or* butter and chopped herbs. Hand croûtons separately.

Potato and leek cream soup

POTAGE PARMENTIER

POTATO AND LEEK CREAM SOUP

Preparation time 15 minutes
Cooking time 30 minutes
To serve 4

You will need

12 oz. leeks *or* 4 oz. onion
1½ oz. butter
12 oz. potatoes, peeled and sliced
1 pint (U.S. 2½ cups) water *or* chicken stock
salt and white pepper
¼ pint (U. S. ⅝ cup) milk
3 tablespoons double cream *or* 1 oz. butter
GARNISH
chopped chives *or* parsley
croûtons (see page 21)

Wash leeks, discard green leaves and slice remainder or slice onion. Melt butter in pan and add leeks *or* onion and potatoes; stir until coated with butter. Cover and cook over *low* heat for 5 minutes. Add water *or* chicken stock and seasoning, cover and simmer for 20 minutes. Sieve and return to pan. All this can be done in advance. Before serving stir in milk and bring just to boiling point. Off heat stir in cream, check seasoning. Serve sprinkled with herbs and hand croûtons separately.

VARIATIONS
POTAGE DE SANTÉ
HEALTH SOUP WITH SORREL

Add 3 oz. shredded sorrel softened in butter to

the finished soup, enrich with an egg yolk and sprinkle with chopped chervil.

POTAGE AU CRESSON
WATERCRESS SOUP

Cook a bunch of watercress with the leeks and potatoes for 5 minutes before sieving. Float a few leaves of watercress on the finished soup.

POTAGE DE TOMATES ET POMMES DE TERRE
TOMATO AND POTATO SOUP

Add 8 oz. peeled and sliced tomatoes to the leek and potatoes and cook for 2 minutes before adding the water.

POT-AU-FEU

BOILED BEEF AND BROTH

Preparation time 15 minutes
Cooking time about 3½ hours
To serve 6

You will need

2 lb. piece lean beef (silverside, shoulder or top rib)
1½–2 lb. knuckle of veal *or* shin of beef (meat and bone)
set chicken giblets, if available
6 pints (U.S. 15 cups) water
4 large carrots, quartered
2 large turnips, quartered
4 leeks, cleaned and trimmed
1 large onion, unpeeled
1 outside stick celery
1 clove
bouquet garni
salt and pepper
TO ACCOMPANY SOUP
bread croûtes (see page 21)
TO ACCOMPANY MEAT
pickled gherkins, French mustard

In large French families a pot-au-feu simmering at the side of the stove is a familiar sight. It provides both a meat course (the bouilli) with vegetables, and excellent broth (the bouillon). The left-overs form the basis of a meal for to-morrow. Tie the meat into a neat shape, and put with the knuckle *or* shin, bones, giblets, etc. into a large stock pot or saucepan. Add cold water and bring *slowly* to the boil. Remove scum as it rises. Add prepared vegetables, clove, bouquet garni and 1 level tablespoon

24

salt. When boiling, skim, then cover and simmer very gently (the liquid should just 'move' not bubble) for 3—3½ hours. Dish drained meat, surround with vegetables and moisten with a little stock; keep warm. Strain broth through a fine sieve into a clean pan, skim off surface fat and 'blot' up remainder with absorbent paper. Check seasoning and reheat. If preferred keep strained broth in a cold place until next day when fat, now solid, can be removed in one piece before reheating the broth. With the soup serve plenty of bread croûtes, and with the meat pickled gherkins and French mustard. Next day remaining cold meat can be sliced for a Beef and Potato Salad (see page 109).

Cream of onion soup

VELOUTÉ D'OIGNON
CREAM OF ONION SOUP

Preparation time   10 minutes
Cooking time   30 minutes
To serve   4

You will need

1 oz. butter
8 oz. onions, *finely* chopped
2 level tablespoons cornflour
2 pints (U.S. 5 cups) milk and water mixed
2 egg yolks
3 tablespoons cream
salt, pepper and nutmeg to season
GARNISH
bread croûtes (see page 21)
grated cheese

Melt the butter in a saucepan and over *low* heat fry the onions until soft but uncoloured. Stir in the cornflour and cook for a minute then stir in the milk and water and simmer for 20 minutes. Beat the egg yolks and cream together, stir in about one third of the soup, then return all to the pan and reheat gently, *without boiling*, and stirring continuously. Season to taste. Sprinkle the bread croûtes with grated cheese and brown lightly under the grill. Float one in each soup bowl.

POTAGE ST. GERMAIN
FRESH PEA SOUP

Preparation time   5–15 minutes
Cooking time   20 minutes
To serve   3–4

You will need

1 leek
2 oz. butter
6 outside lettuce leaves, shredded
1 lb. shelled peas, fresh *or* frozen
1 teaspoon salt
½ teaspoon sugar
1¼ pints (U.S. 3⅛ cups) water
GARNISH
a few cooked peas

Wash and slice the leek. Melt 1½ oz. of the butter in a saucepan over a *low* heat and add the prepared leek, lettuce and peas, salt and sugar. Stir to mix thoroughly together with the butter, then cover and cook gently for 5 minutes. Add the water and simmer, covered, until tender, for 10—15 minutes depending on maturity of peas. Reserve a few peas for garnishing then sieve or purée the soup. Return the puréed soup to the saucepan, reheat and check the seasoning. Off the heat stir in the remaining butter.
Serve garnished with the reserved peas.

SOUPE DE POISSON

FISH SOUP

(Illustrated in colour on page 20)
Preparation time 15 minutes
Cooking time 45 minutes
To serve 4

You will need

3 oz. onions
3 oz. leeks
1 carrot
4 tablespoons olive oil
2 cloves garlic, crushed
8 oz. ripe tomatoes, quartered
   or 8 oz. can peeled tomatoes
2 pints (U.S. 5 cups) water
bouquet fresh herbs — parsley, basil, fennel,
   thyme
large pinch saffron
2 teaspoons salt
2 lb. fresh cod *or* haddock, including head and
   bones
1 oz. spaghetti *or* vermicelli in 1-inch pieces
GARNISH
croûtes of French bread (see page 21)
grated Gruyère *or* Parmesan cheese

Prepare and thinly slice the onions, leeks and
carrot. Heat the oil in a large saucepan and fry
the vegetables gently until soft but uncoloured,
about 5 minutes. Add the garlic and tomatoes and
cook for 5 minutes longer. Add the water, herbs,
saffron and salt. Cut the fish into thick slices, add
to the pan and boil gently, uncovered, for 35 minutes. Press through a strainer and return broth to
the pan. When boiling add the pasta and cook for
10 minutes or until tender. Check seasoning. Place
the bread croûtes (treated with oil and garlic, see
page 21) in a tureen or in soup plates and pour
the boiling soup over. Hand grated cheese separately.
Note
This soup has the savour of a Mediterranean fish
soup although made with white fish.

POTAGE BONNE FEMME

'GOOD WOMAN' VEGETABLE SOUP

Preparation time 20 minutes
Cooking time 30 minutes
To serve 4

You will need

2 large leeks
1½ oz. butter
2 large carrots, diced
1 lb. potatoes, diced
1 stick tender celery, sliced
1½ pints (U.S. 3¾ cups) water
salt and sugar to season
3 tablespoons double cream
GARNISH
1 tablespoon finely chopped parsley *or* chervil

Clean leeks, discard dark green leaves and slice
remainder. Melt butter in a saucepan, add prepared leeks and carrots and stir over a gentle heat
until they have absorbed the butter. (This is the
secret of good vegetable soups.) Stir in prepared
potatoes and celery. Add water and seasonings,
cover, and simmer for 25—30 minutes, until tender.
Sieve, return to rinsed pan and reheat. If necessary
thin with a little milk and adjust seasoning. Just
before serving stir in cream and herbs.

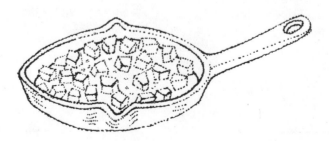

Potage bonne femme ('Good woman' vegetable soup)

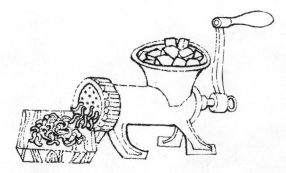

PÂTÉS AND TERRINES
PATÉS ET TERRINES

The word pâté has an aura of luxury — and the truffled confections of top restaurants are really sumptuous. But the delicious everyday 'pâté maison' or 'terrine du chef' found in local bistros and cooked meat shops (charcuterie) throughout France are neither expensive nor extravagant.

These simple pâtés are not at all difficult to make at home and every cook can create his or her very own 'pâté maison' after a few trial runs. The basic formula is always a mixture of minced meats in which lean meats such as veal, liver, poultry or game are judiciously blended with fat meat — usually in the form of belly pork, bacon or strips of back pork fat. The amount of seasoning, garlic, herbs, wine and spices you add is a matter of personal taste so experiment with a basic mixture

until you get it to your liking. One word of warning — pâtés containing wine and spirits seem to emphasise the flavour of garlic so use only half a clove until you're sure.

Incidentally the addition of wines and spirits is not essential but they are largely responsible for those subtle flavours we associate with French pâtés.

The texture can be rough or smooth depending on how finely you choose to mince the meats. Mincing raw meat sometimes poses a problem but a friendly butcher when not too busy will often do it for you. Nowadays the terms pâté and terrine are both applied to a mixture of meats baked in an ovenproof dish. A similar mixture baked in a pastry case is known as a 'pâté en croûte'.

GENERAL NOTES ON MAKING PÂTÉS

THE DISH

Traditionally a round or oval earthenware dish with straight sides and a lid with a hole in it. In practise any ovenproof pie dish, casserole or soufflé case will do. If it has no lid cover with foil whilst baking. For a pâté en croûte or a jellied pâté a large loaf tin is suitable.

LINING THE DISH

Lean mixtures are often packed into bacon lined dishes. For this use unsmoked bacon, or very *mild* smoked bacon. Stretch thin rashers even thinner by elongating with a heavy knife (see page 10). Non-lined dishes usually have strips of fat bacon laid over the surface.

PRESSING

Many recipes tell you to press the cooked pâté

with a heavy weight. This is not essential but will give a closer, easier to slice texture if the pâté is to be turned out.

COOKING 'AU BAIN-MARIE'

A bain-marie is simply a water bath to ensure slow moist cooking. Stand the pâté in a baking tin filled with hot water to reach half way up the dish. Timing varies according to the depth of mixture and size of dish.

KEEPING

Pâtés are at their best if 'matured' for 3 days before eating. Kept covered in a refrigerator pâtés will keep for at least a week and are a great standby. Allow to regain room temperature before serving.

SERVING

Usually pâtés are served as the first course of a formal meal but can be a meal in themselves for a family supper. Serve them from the terrine either sliced or spooned according to texture, or turned out and cut in thick slices. Serve with freshly made hot thin toast or crusty French bread, and creamy unsalted butter.

TERRINE AUX AROMATES
HERB PÂTÉ

Preparation time 20–30 minutes
Cooking time 1 hour
To serve 4

You will need

1 lb. spinach *or* 10 oz. carton frozen spinach
1 lb. lean belly pork, minced
4 oz. cooked ham, diced
1 heaped tablespoon mixed chopped fresh herbs
 (parsley, chervil, basil, marjoram, etc.)
2 oz. onion, finely grated
½ clove garlic, crushed
1 level teaspoon salt
ground black pepper
¼ level teaspoon grated nutmeg
1 egg
4 rashers mild streaky bacon

A rough textured green flecked and herb flavoured pâté.
Cook prepared fresh or the frozen spinach in boiling

Herb pâté

salted water, drain and press as dry as possible. Chop finely or mince with the pork. Into a basin put the spinach, pork, ham, herbs, onion, garlic, salt, pepper, nutmeg and egg. Mix *very thoroughly*. Press into a 1½-pint capacity ovenproof dish. Remove the rind from the rashers of bacon and lay them on top of the mixture in the dish. Cover and stand in a baking tin with hot water to reach halfway up the dish. Cook in centre of a pre-heated moderate oven (350 °F. or Gas Mark 4), for about 1 hour. When cold, cover and mature in refrigerator for 24 hours.
Serve from the terrine, garnished with olives and herbs when available.

PATÉ DE CAMPAGNE
COUNTRY PÂTÉ

(Illustrated in colour on frontispiece)
Preparation time 20 minutes
Cooking time 1¼–1½ hours
To serve 6–8

You will need

8 oz. lean veal
8 oz. fresh belly pork
4 oz. cooked ham
4 oz. pigs liver
½ clove garlic
4 oz. back pork fat, diced
1 level teaspoon salt
¼ teaspoon ground black pepper
⅛ teaspoon ground allspice *or* mace
4 tablespoons white wine *or* brandy
piece of flare fat *or* 3 rashers fat bacon,
 rind removed

This is a savoury rough texture country pâté. Mince coarsely the veal, belly pork, ham and liver. Crush the garlic and add with the diced pork fat, salt and pepper, allspice *or* mace and wine *or* spirit to the veal mixture. Mix *very thoroughly*. Pack into 1½-pint capacity ovenproof dish, doming the top. Place flare fat *or* rindless rashers on top, then cover with lid or kitchen foil. Allow to stand 1—2 hours. Place in baking tin with hot water to reach halfway up the dish and bake in centre of a pre-heated moderate oven (350°F. or Gas Mark 4), for 1¼—1½ hours.

TERRINE TANTE MARIE

TANTE MARIE TERRINE

Preparation time 30 minutes
Cooking time about 1¼ hours
To serve 4–6

You will need

6–8 thin rashers unsmoked streaky bacon
half a young rabbit *or* chicken
4 oz. pigs liver
4 oz. fresh pork
4 oz. sausage meat
2 oz. onion, grated
1 tablespoon finely chopped parsley
1 oz. bread soaked in milk
2 tablespoons brandy
1 small egg, beaten
salt, pepper and grated nutmeg
2 bay leaves

Line the inside of a 1½-pint terrine with bacon
rashers. Remove flesh from rabbit *or* chicken and
cut into thin slices. With a sharp knife chop the
liver and pork very finely, put into a basin and
add sausage meat, onion, parsley, bread previously
squeezed dry, brandy, egg and liberal seasonings
of salt, pepper and nutmeg. Beat together very
thoroughly. Spread a layer of this farce in bottom
of lined terrine, lay slices of rabbit on top, then
a layer of farce, a layer of rabbit, ending with farce.
Place a rasher of bacon and a bay leaf on top and
cover with greaseproof paper and the lid. Stand
in baking tin half full of hot water and cook in a
pre-heated moderate oven (350°F. or Gas Mark 4),
for about 1¼ hours. Cool a little then place weight
on top and leave until cold. Will keep in refrigerator
for a week. Put a fresh bay leaf on top and serve
from the terrine.

PATÉ DE FOIE DU PORC

LIVER PÂTÉ

Preparation time 15 minutes
Cooking time about 1–1¼ hours
To serve 4–6

You will need

8 oz. pigs liver
8 oz. fresh belly pork, boned
½ clove garlic
2 tablespoons dry white wine *or* brandy
2 level teaspoons salt
1 level teaspoon ground black pepper
3 rashers streaky bacon

This is the simplest pâté of all, rich and satisfying.
Mince the liver and pork fairly coarsely. Crush
garlic very finely and add with wine *or* brandy,
salt and pepper to the minced liver and pork. Mix
very thoroughly and press into a 1-pint sized ovenproof terrine. Cut the bacon into thin strips and
criss cross over the surface. Cover, and if possible
leave for 2 hours for flavours to blend before
baking. Stand in a baking tin with hot water to
reach halfway up dish and cook in centre of a pre-

Tante Marie terrine
Cooking the terrine 'au bain-marie'

Tante Marie terrine
The finished dish

heated moderate oven, (335°F. or Gas Mark 3), for 1—1¼ hours. Remove cover for the last 10 minutes of cooking time. When cold, cover and refrigerate for 2—3 days before serving.

TERRINE DE PORC, VEAU ET JAMBON

TERRINE OF PORK, VEAL AND HAM

Preparation time 30 minutes
Cooking time about 1½ hours
To serve 8–10

You will need

6 oz. slice fillet of veal, ¼-inch thick
2 tablespoons brandy
salt and ground black pepper
4 oz. thin rashers unsmoked bacon
6 oz. slice lean cooked ham
1 oz. butter
3 tablespoons finely chopped onion
6 tablespoons Madeira, port *or* brandy
1 lb. fresh belly pork, finely minced
12 oz. lean pie veal, finely minced
2 small eggs
large pinch allspice
¼ teaspoon dried thyme
½ clove garlic, crushed
1 bay leaf

A terrine from the 'haute cuisine' class.
Cut the veal into ¼-inch strips and marinate with the brandy and a little seasoning while preparing the other ingredients. Remove rinds from rashers of bacon and use to line a 2½-pint terrine. Cut the lean cooked ham into ¼-inch thick strips.
Prepare the farce mixture as follows: — melt the butter and fry the onion gently until soft but not coloured. Add wine *or* spirit and bubble briskly until reduced by half. Add minced pork and veal, beaten eggs, salt, pepper, allspice, thyme and garlic, and the brandy drained from the strips of veal. Beat vigorously until well mixed. Divide the mixture into three. Spread one third in the bottom of the lined terrine and lay drained veal strips on top. Cover with farce then strips of ham and a final layer of farce. Lay bay leaf and the remainder of the bacon rashers on top. Cover with kitchen foil and a lid. Stand in baking tin with hot water to reach halfway up the dish. Cook for about 1½ hours in centre of a pre-heated moderate oven, (350°F. or Gas Mark 4).
Weight while cooling. Leave to mature for 3 days, in the refrigerator.
Serve from the terrine, or turn out and garnish with watercress.

Note

For a very special Game Pâté replace the veal and ham by 12 oz. raw skinless game cut into strips. Use pheasant, duck, hare, partridge, rabbit *or* other game, in season.

PATÉ EN CROUTE

PÂTÉ IN A PASTRY CRUST

Preparation time 1 hour
Cooking time   2 hours
To serve   8

You will need

PASTRY
1 lb. plain flour
2 level teaspoons salt
8 oz. margarine *or* butter
about ¼ pint (U.S. ⅝ cup) cold water
FILLING
1¼ lb. boneless pie veal
6 oz. belly pork
2 eggs, beaten
1 tablespoon brandy
salt and pepper
1 slice cooked ham ½-inch thick
2 thin slices ham fat, same size as ham

To make pastry, sift the flour and salt, rub in the fat and mix to a stiff dough with water. Form pastry into a ball and smear a little at a time along table with palm of hand (known as the fraisage, see picture page 130). Reform ball and repeat twice more. Chill for 1—2 hours before using. When ready roll out two-thirds of dough and line a greased large bread tin or oblong mould. Press

Pâté in a pastry crust

pastry to bottom and sides of tin and trim ¼-inch above top edge. Prepare filling as follows. Coarsely mince veal and pork and mix with eggs, brandy, salt and pepper. Sandwich ham between the slices of fat and cut into 4 strips. Spread one third of filling in bottom of lined mould, lay strips of ham and fat on top, cover with filling, then remaining ham and cover with remaining filling. Roll rest of pastry to fit top, trim, and seal edges together. Decorate with rounds of pastry and pierce a hole in centre of each to allow steam to escape; keep open with a roll of paper. Brush with beaten egg and cook in a pre-heated moderate oven, (350°F. or Gas Mark 4), for about 2 hours reducing heat towards end if necessary. Serve hot, or reheat in a slow oven when required.

FROMAGE DE PORC

JELLIED PORK LOAF

Preparation time 20 minutes
Cooking time   3 hours
To serve   8

You will need

5 lb. hand of pork including trotter
¼ pint (U.S. ⅝ cup) dry white wine
1 onion, peeled
1 large carrot, peeled and quartered
1 stick celery, cut up
1 tomato, quartered
1 bay leaf
strip lemon peel
several stalks of parsley
6 peppercorns
2 level teaspoons salt

Ask the butcher to remove the pork rind and split the trotter in half. Put the meat, rind and trotter into a large deep pan with all the other ingredients. Add sufficient cold water to cover and bring slowly to the boil. Skim, cover closely and barely simmer for 2½—3 hours. Remove meat. Strain stock through a muslin lined colander, return to the pan and boil rapidly until reduced by half. Cut the meat into 1-inch cubes, discarding bone and gristle, and pack into a wetted 2-lb. loaf tin. Check seasoning of reduced stock and pour over meat. Leave in a cold place until set and jellied.
Serve unmoulded and garnished with salad vege-

Jellied pork loaf

tables. Cut in thick slices and offer a mustard flavoured mayonnaise separately (see page 119).

Note

Garlic lovers can add a handful of parsley chopped finely with 2 cloves garlic to the stock before pouring over the meat.
This is a Burgundian touch.

RILLETTES DE PORC

A SOFT POTTED PORK

Preparation time 10 minutes
Cooking time 4 hours
To serve 6

You will need

1 lb. lean fillet pork
1 lb. fat belly pork
salt and ground black pepper
1 clove garlic, peeled (optional)
1 bay leaf
1 sprig thyme
water

A rich soft potted pork, a regional dish from Normandy and Touraine.
Cut the meat and fat into 1-inch cubes. Put into a flameproof casserole with salt, pepper, garlic (if used), bay leaf, thyme and water just to cover. Cook, covered, over *very low* heat until the water evaporates and the meat is *very* soft. This will take

about 3—4 hours but should water evaporate sooner add a little more. During cooking press meat against sides of casserole now and then. Drain off the fat and reserve. Remove any bones. Using two forks mash and pull the meat apart until reduced literally to shreds. Check seasoning. Press into individual pots and cover each with some of the strained fat. Will keep, covered in the refrigerator for 1 week.

TERRINE DE GIBIER

GAME PÂTÉ

Preparation time 30 minutes, plus overnight to marinate
Cooking time about 1½ hours
To serve 4–6

You will need

1 lb. duck *or* pigeon flesh, without bone*
8 oz. fresh belly pork
1 tablespoon brandy
2 tablespoons Madeira
1 tablespoon orange juice
2 oz. grated onion
½ level teaspoon dried herbs
salt and pepper
1 egg, beaten
4 oz. thin rashers unsmoked bacon

* *or* partridge, pheasant, hare *or* other game

Mince the game and pork, add the brandy, Madeira, orange juice, onion, herbs and seasoning, mix well and leave to marinate in refrigerator overnight.
Next day add the egg and beat thoroughly. Remove the rind from the bacon rashers and line a 1½-pint capacity terrine with the bacon, press in the mixture and lay remaining rashers on top. Cover with lid or foil and stand in baking tin filled with hot water to reach halfway up the dish. Cook in a pre-heated moderate oven (350°F. or Gas Mark 4), for 1¼—1½ hours. Allow to mature for 3 days in the refrigerator before serving.

PATÉ DE FOIES DE VOLAILLES

CHICKEN LIVER PÂTÉ

Preparation time 15 minutes plus 2 hours to marinate
Cooking time about 1¼ hours
To serve 6–8

You will need

12 oz. chicken livers
2 tablespoons Madeira, port *or* brandy
2 tablespoons white wine
1 crumbled bay leaf
½ clove garlic, crushed
  or 1 oz. chopped onion
2 oz. slice firm bread, soaked in milk
4 oz. cooked ham
8 oz. pork sausage meat
3–4 oz. thin rashers unsmoked bacon

This is a rich pâté. Wash livers and remove any tissues. Put livers in a basin with wines, bay leaf, and garlic *or* onion and leave for 2 hours. Squeeze the bread dry and put through a fine mincer with the ham, sausage meat and all but 3 of the drained livers. Mix thoroughly and beat in the rest of the wine marinade. The mixture will be fairly soft. Stretch the rindless bacon rashers as thinly as possible with a heavy knife, and line a 1½-pint pie dish, allowing rashers to extend beyond the rim.

Chicken liver pâté
Stretching the bacon rashers

Spread half the liver mixture in the bottom, lay remaining livers, halved, on top, and cover with rest of mixture. Fold bacon rashers over surface and cover dish with foil. Stand in baking tin filled with hot water to reach halfway up dish. Cook in centre of a pre-heated oven (350°F. or Gas Mark 4), for about 1¼ hours. Weight while cooling. Mature for 2—3 days in the refrigerator before turning out and serving in thick slices.

TERRINE DE LAPIN

RABBIT PÂTÉ

Preparation time 30 minutes plus 3–4 hours to marinate
Cooking time about 1½ hours
To serve 6

You will need

1 wild rabbit, about 2 lb.
3 tablespoons brandy *or* dry white wine
1 small onion, sliced
1 bay leaf
salt and ground black pepper
8 oz. pork sausage meat
½ clove garlic, crushed (optional)
3–4 oz. thin rashers unsmoked streaky bacon

Bone the rabbit. Slice meat and marinade with

Chicken liver pâté
Lining the dish with the bacon rashers

brandy *or* wine, onion, bay leaf and seasoning for 3—4 hours, stirring occasionally. Chop heart and liver, mix with sausage meat, garlic (if used) and strained liquid from marinade. Line a 1½-pint terrine with bacon (see photograph on page 34) and in it arrange alternately sausage meat mixture and rabbit. Cover closely and bake as for Liver Pâté (see page 30) for about 1½ hours.

MOUSSE DE FOIES DE VOLAILLE

INDIVIDUAL CHICKEN LIVER MOUSSE

Preparation time 15–20 minutes
Cooking time 5 minutes
To serve 4

You will need

8 oz. chicken livers
1 rounded tablespoon chopped shallot
   or blanched onion
3 oz. butter
cut clove of garlic
3 tablespoons Madeira *or* brandy
3 tablespoons double cream
salt and ground black pepper
large pinch allspice

Chicken liver pâté
Covering the dish with foil

Wash liver, discard membranes and cut into ½-inch pieces. Melt 1 oz. butter and fry shallot *or* onion gently for 1—2 minutes. Add livers and fry 2—3 minutes until stiffened but still pink inside. Turn into a basin previously well rubbed with garlic. Boil Madeira *or* brandy in same pan until well reduced then add to livers with the cream, seasoning and allspice. Either blend at top speed for several seconds in an electric blender until reduced to a smooth paste or press through a fairly fine sieve. Blend or beat in the remaining butter, softened. Check seasoning. Pack into individual cocottes, cover and chill. Serve with fingers of hot, unbuttered, toast.

PATÉ DE POISSON

A FISH PÂTÉ

Put contents of a 7 oz. can of tunny fish *or* salmon, including oil but minus bones, into an electric liquidiser. Add 3 oz. unsalted, slightly softened butter, 2 teaspoons lemon juice and a little ground black pepper. Mix at medium speed until reduced to a smooth purée. Check seasoning and turn into individual pots. Serve with hot unbuttered toast. Will keep for several days in a refrigerator. Soften to room temperature before serving.

Chicken liver pâté
The finished dish

PATÉ EN CROUTE AUX ÉPINARDS

VEAL, HAM AND PORK PIE WITH SPINACH

(Illustrated in colour opposite)

Preparation time 2½ hours, including resting of pastry
Cooking time 2 hours
To serve 12

You will need

FILLING
12 oz. fillet of veal
2–3 tablespoons brandy
2 tablespoons finely chopped onion
1 tablespoon oil
1 lb. raw belly *or* shoulder pork, minced
2 eggs, beaten
⅛ teaspoon powdered allspice
⅛ teaspoon dried thyme
salt and ground black pepper
4 oz. smoked streaky bacon
8 oz. raw spinach leaves, washed
6 oz. sliced cooked ham
a little jellied stock flavoured with Madeira
PASTRY
1 lb. plain flour
2 level teaspoons salt
2 oz. lard
5 oz. butter
1 egg, beaten
about 6 tablespoons cold water
GLAZE
little beaten egg

Cut the veal into thin slices and cover with the brandy. Leave to marinate until required.

TO MAKE THE PASTRY:

Sift the flour and salt into a mixing bowl and rub in the lard and butter *coarsely*. Add the beaten egg and the water; mix to a dough and 'smear' little by little across pastry board as for 'fraisage' (see illustration on page 130).
Gather into a ball, wrap in greaseproof paper and chill for 2 hours.

TO MAKE THE FILLING:

Fry the finely chopped onion *gently* in oil until soft but not coloured; add the minced pork, the beaten eggs, allspice, thyme and a generous seasoning of salt and black pepper. Just before using add the brandy from veal and mix all thoroughly together. Line a 2-lb. mould with two thirds of the pastry. In it arrange alternate layers of farce, veal, bacon, spinach and ham until all are used. Roll out the remaining pastry large enough to cover the top. Damp the edges with water and place over the filling, sealing dampened edges firmly. Decorate with two pastry circles and pierce a hole in the centre of each to allow the steam to escape; keep the hole open with a twist of foil.

TO GLAZE:

Brush with the beaten egg and cook in the centre of a pre-heated moderate oven (350°F. or Gas Mark 4), for 1 hour.
Reduce heat to (335°F. or Gas Mark 3), and cook for a further hour protecting the top with foil or greaseproof paper, if necessary, to prevent over browning. When cooked remove twists of foil or greaseproof paper and pour a little melted stock through the holes. Serve cold with a green salad.

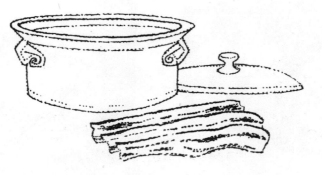

Pâté en croûte aux épinards (Veal, ham and pork pie with spinach)

Oeufs sur canapés (Eggs, ham and cheese on bread)

There is some kind of divine affinity between the flavour of a mild cured ham and the type of cheese we know as Gruyère. The French combine them in a hundred different ways. Often you will find them sandwiched between bread and fried golden in butter — a savoury morsel known throughout France as Croque Monsieur. Sometimes in Savoy a thick slice of ham sits in a slice on a canapé of puff pastry shrouded in a blanket of mornay sauce and a thick layer of toasted Gruyère.

In our picture the ham and cheese are combined with an egg and a crisp buttery croûton to provide a delectable savoury snack. And incidentally this is yet another way to add to the Frenchman's 600 ways of cooking an egg.

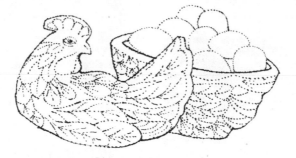

EGGS

LES OEUFS

The French do not serve eggs for breakfast but they *do* have over 600 different ways of cooking them. They also have the enviable knack of giving a simple basic recipe, such as eggs baked in individual dishes (see page 40) a different look each time they serve them, simply by adding a few mushrooms, a slice of foie gras or other ingredients. The popular time for serving eggs in France is as a first course for luncheon. Hard-boiled eggs are combined with mayonnaise, and either anchovies,

tunny fish, shrimps or tomatoes. Soft-boiled eggs cooked so that the whites are firm but the yolks remain soft (see Oeufs Mollet page 42) are served cold in meat jelly (Oeufs en Gelée) or hot and veiled with a delectable sauce. Eggs are used extensively too in custards, ices and in sweet and savoury flans.

We are deeply indebted to French skill with eggs for the invention of the omelette and the soufflé.

OEUFS EN GELÉE

EGGS IN TARRAGON FLAVOURED JELLY

Preparation time   25 minutes plus time to cool jelly
Cooking time   10 minutes
To serve   4

You will need

4 soft-boiled eggs (see Oeufs Mollet page 42)
1½ level teaspoons (scant ¼ oz.) gelatine
½ pint (U.S. 1¼ cups) clear consommé, fresh or canned
1–2 teaspoons tarragon vinegar
1 tablespoon Madeira or port
2 oz. cooked ham, chopped
few tarragon leaves to decorate

Shell the eggs and leave them in cold water until

required. Sprinkle the gelatine into the cold consommé, allow to soften for 2—3 minutes then stir over gentle heat until completely dissolved. Stir in the tarragon vinegar (*or* wine vinegar plus a chopped sprig tarragon), and the Madeira or port.

Set aside until cold but still liquid. Divide the ham between 4 individual cocotte dishes. Drain and dry the eggs and put one in each dish. Pour in the jelly (strained if necessary) just to cover and decorate each with tarragon leaves.

When set stand the cocottes on small plates and serve with a teaspoon.

Note

The exact timing of the eggs for the dish is important as the yolk should remain soft while the white is just set.

Eggs with mushrooms and cream

OEUFS EN COCOTTE

EGGS POACHED
OR BAKED IN INDIVIDUAL DISHES

Preparation time 2 minutes
Cooking time 4–8 minutes
To serve 1

You will need

¼ oz. butter
1 fresh egg
1 tablespoon cream (optional)
salt and pepper

A simple way of cooking one or more eggs. Place cocotte with butter inside, in a shallow pan containing *gently* simmering water to reach halfway up. When dish hot and butter melted break in egg and spoon cream over the surface. Cover pan with a lid and cook 4—6 minutes on top of the cooker, or in a pre-heated moderate oven (375°F. or Gas Mark 5), for 6—8 minutes. The white should be lightly set and the yolk soft.
Sprinkle with salt and pepper and serve at once in the cocotte. Eat with a teaspoon.

VARIATIONS

OEUFS COCOTTE AUX FINES HERBES
EGGS WITH HERBS AND CREAM

Add a tablespoon of mixed chopped fresh chives, tarragon and parsley to the cream before cooking.

OEUFS COCOTTE AU JAMBON
EGGS WITH HAM AND CREAM

Heat ½ oz. finely shredded cooked ham in the butter before adding the egg and cream.

OEUFS COCOTTE BERGÈRE
EGGS WITH MUSHROOMS AND CREAM

Fry 1 oz. finely chopped mushrooms and a little parsley in 1 oz. butter *or* margarine; season, and put in bottom of cocotte before adding the egg and cream.

OEUFS DURS A LA TRIPE

HARD-BOILED EGGS
IN ONION SAUCE

Preparation time 10 minutes
Cooking time 20 minutes
To serve 4

You will need

1 oz. butter
8 oz. onions, sliced
2 level tablespoons cornflour
¾ pint (U.S. 3⅛ cups) milk
salt and pepper
5 hard-boiled eggs
GARNISH
browned onion rings *or* chopped parsley

Melt the butter in a saucepan and very gently sauté the onions until soft but not browned. Stir in the cornflour, mixing well. Off the heat gradually stir in all the milk then return to the heat, stir until boiling, and simmer for 10 minutes. Season

Hard-boiled eggs in onion sauce

to taste. Cut the eggs length-wise into eight, reserve one for garnish and stir remainder gently into the sauce. Turn into one large dish (or 4 small cocottes) and garnish with reserved egg slices and either browned onion rings *or* chopped parsley.

OMELETTE AU NATUREL
SAVOURY OMELETTE

Preparation time 2 minutes
Cooking time   about 1 minute
To serve   1

You will need

2 eggs
1 tablespoon cold water
salt and pepper to taste
½ oz. butter

Omelettes are so quick and simple to make therefore no one should be without the only essential item of equipment which is a pan kept exclusively for omelettes.
You will need a 6—7 inch pan for a 2 egg omelette or 9—10 inch pan for a 4 egg, (2 portion) omelette. A heavy pan with non-stick surface is ideal.
With a fork lightly beat the eggs with the water and salt and pepper, enough to mix, but no more. Heat the pan thoroughly, add the butter and when on the point of turning nut brown pour in the lightly beaten egg mixture. Holding the handle in the left hand and fork in the right hand, cook the omelette over *high* heat, tilting the pan forward and back at the same time lifting the 'set' portion of the omelette from the bottom of the pan with the fork to allow the raw egg to run underneath and cook. When lightly set but still a little runny on the surface, tilt the pan away from you and roll the omelette to the far side. Allow to brown for a second or two then tilt the pan so that the omelette rolls out in a fat cigar shape onto a hot dish. *Serve at once.*
The cooking should take less than a minute and the omelette should be golden brown outside and creamy in the centre.

LES OMELETTES FARCIES
STUFFED OMELETTES

No one should ever tire of omelettes because there are so many ways of varying the flavour either by additions to the raw mixture **or** by filling the cooked omelette. Fillings are sometimes spooned across the omelette just *before* rolling or folding; or the rolled omelette is split and filled down the centre, after turning out.

OMELETTE FINES HERBES
HERB OMELETTE

Add to the raw egg mixture 1 tablespoon of mixed finely chopped fresh herbs — parsley, chives, tarragon and chervil if possible.

OMELETTE AU FROMAGE
CHEESE OMELETTE

Add 1 level tablespoon each grated Parmesan and Gruyère to the raw egg mixture. When omelette is half cooked spoon over 1 tablespoon thick cream, then fold and serve.

OMELETTE AUX CROUTONS
FRIED BREAD OMELETTE

Cut a thick slice of bread into ¼-inch dice. Fry slowly in butter, turning frequently until evenly brown and crisp. Slit cooked omelette and fill with the croûtons.

OEUFS SUR LE PLAT
EGGS COOKED AND SERVED IN THE SAME DISH

For this practical French version of fried eggs you need a special individual flameproof dish (see page 10). Melt ¼ oz. butter in the dish over *low* heat. Break one or two eggs separately into a saucer and slide into the dish. Cover with a saucepan lid. Cook just until the yolk is filmed with white, about 1 minute on top of cooker *or* 4 minutes in a preheated moderate oven, (350°F. or Gas Mark 4). Serve immediately.

OEUFS SUR CANAPÉS

EGGS, HAM AND CHEESE ON BREAD

(Illustrated in colour on page 38)
Preparation time 5 minutes
Cooking time 12–15 minutes
To serve 1

You will need

¾ oz. butter
1 large slice bread, ½-inch thick
1 small egg
1 oz. ham, chopped
1 oz. Gruyère cheese, grated

Pre-heat oven to (350°F. or Gas Mark 4). Melt butter in frying pan and pass bread through it (without frying) so that both sides are well buttered. Place bread on baking sheet and deeply hollow the surface with back of a spoon. Carefully break egg into hollow. Sprinkle with ham and then with cheese to cover egg completely. Bake for 12—15 minutes. Serve at once. If you don't mind a hard skin on the egg bake with ham and cheese at either end, as in the photograph.

OEUFS MOLLET

FIVE MINUTE BOILED EGGS

Only very fresh eggs can be used. Lower eggs into *gently* boiling water to cover and when water regains simmering point time for exactly 5 minutes for standard 2 oz. size eggs.
Immediately drain off water and cover eggs with fresh *cold* water to stop further cooking.
After 5 minutes remove shell by cradling egg in the hand and tapping gently all over with back of spoon; peel away cracked shell. Keep the shelled eggs submerged in *warm* water for serving hot or in *cold* water if to be served cold.

VARIATION
OEUFS MOLLET A LA FLORENTINE
FIVE MINUTE BOILED EGGS WITH SPINACH

Make ½ pint Mornay sauce (see page 121). Cook large carton frozen spinach, press dry. Add 2—3 tablespoons sauce; place in bottom of gratin dish. Season. Set 3 or 4 oeufs mollet on top. Coat with remaining sauce; sprinkle with cheese and brown lightly under the grill.

LA PIPERADE DU PAYS BASQUE

HAM AND EGGS BASQUE STYLE

Preparation time 20 minutes
Cooking time 25–30 minutes
To serve 4

You will need

1 lb. ripe tomatoes, skinned and halved
3 tablespoons olive oil
1 onion, finely chopped
1 clove garlic, crushed (optional)
2 sweet green peppers, deseeded and flesh cut into thin strips
salt and sugar to season
4 small gammon rashers
4 eggs, lightly beaten
chopped parsley

Remove seeds from tomatoes and roughly chop pulp. Heat oil in frying pan and fry onion, garlic and pepper *very gently* for about 15 minutes. Add tomatoes and seasoning; cook *gently* until most of liquid has evaporated and tomatoes are reduced to a pulp. Meanwhile grill or fry gammon rashers. Add eggs to vegetables and stir over gentle heat until eggs are lightly scrambled. Serve at once in a shallow dish, with gammon rashers on top sprinkled with parsley.

La Piperade du pays Basque (Ham and eggs Basque style)

CHEESES
FROMAGES

France produces about three hundred different cheeses offering an enormous variety of flavours, textures, sizes and shapes. Although many are produced commercially and exported, others are local cheeses well worth seeking out to enjoy with the local 'vin du pays' when travelling through France. With one or two exceptions French cheeses are for eating rather than cooking.

In a formal meal cheese in France is served *after* the meat and salad but *before* the sweet or dessert. An excellent custom this as wines served with earlier courses can be finished with the cheese thus cleansing the palate and paving the way for the pudding and dessert wine to follow.

For an informal meal an assortment of cheeses arranged on a large wooden platter, with black grapes and apples or pears, is a feast of which few people ever tire. With the cheese board serve chunks of crusty French bread, creamy Normandy butter and one or more wines. Brief notes on the various types of cheese, hints on buying and storing and suggested wines to serve are given opposite the colour picture on page 47.

For cooking, the French use Gruyère or Emmental, and Italian Parmesan. These cheeses, dry and grated, and used in equal proportions, impart a subtle flavour which harmonises perfectly with wine. In classical recipes you find them used time and time again, for Mornay sauce, for cheese gratins, for soufflés and so on. Other typically French recipes using cheese can be found in the chapter on Savoury Pastry.

SOUFFLÉ AU FROMAGE
CHEESE SOUFFLÉ

Preparation time 20 minutes
Cooking time 25–30 minutes
To serve 4

You will need

1½ oz. butter
1 oz. flour
½ pint (U.S. 1¼ cups) milk less 4 tablespoons
2 oz. finely grated Parmesan cheese
1–2 oz. finely grated Gruyère cheese
4 eggs, separated
salt, pepper and dry mustard,

Butter a 1½-pint soufflé case and place on a baking sheet. Pre-heat an oven to (375°F. or Gas Mark 5). Melt the butter in a medium-sized saucepan, stir in the flour, add the milk and whisk with a small wire whisk until smooth and boiling. Simmer for 3—4 minutes then remove from the heat. Beat in the cheese, the egg yolks one at a time, and seasoning to taste. (This basic mixture can be made in advance). Whisk the egg whites until stiff but not dry and stir one large tablespoonful into the mixture. Fold in the remainder lightly and quickly with a metal spoon. Immediately turn into prepared dish. Bake in centre of pre-heated oven for 25—30 minutes or until lightly set and golden brown.

Serve *at once* in the dish, as a first course, or as a savoury.

Cheese soufflé

Cream cheese and bacon flan

TARTE AU FROMAGE BLANC
CREAM CHEESE
AND BACON FLAN

Preparation time 30 minutes
Cooking time 20–25 minutes
To serve 4–5

You will need

6 oz. rich flan pastry (see page 130)
4 oz. mild smoked streaky bacon rashers
3 packets Demi-sel *or* 6 oz. unsalted cream
   cheese
2 large eggs
$\frac{1}{4}$ pint (U.S. $\frac{5}{8}$ cup) single cream
salt and pepper

Make the pastry, roll out and line an 8-inch flan ring.
Pre-heat an oven to (375°F. or Gas Mark 5). Remove rinds from bacon and cut into 1-inch strips. Fry them in a dry pan just until the fat runs; keep aside. Mash the Demi-sel *or* cream cheese, add the eggs and beat with a wire whisk until smooth. Beat in the cream and light seasonings of salt and pepper. Arrange the bacon strips over the base of the flan and pour in the cream cheese mixture. Bake in the centre of the pre-heated oven for 25—30 minutes. If already golden brown cover with greaseproof paper and continue cooking another 10 minutes or until filling is set in the centre.
This flan is good served hot, warm or cold, alone as a first course, or with salad for a luncheon or picnic.

LE GRATIN LANDAIS
POTATO, HAM
AND CHEESE DISH

Preparation time 15 minutes
Cooking time 1$\frac{1}{4}$–1$\frac{1}{2}$ hours
To serve 3–4

You will need

1 lb. waxy type potatoes, peeled
3 oz. grated Gruyère cheese
6 oz. thinly sliced raw gammon, diced
ground black pepper to taste
$\frac{1}{3}$ pint (U.S. $\frac{7}{8}$ cup) milk
3 tablespoons double cream

Slice potatoes *very* thinly. In a buttered gratin dish arrange alternate layers of potatoes, cheese, gammon and seasoning, ending with potatoes. Pour the mixed milk and cream over and bake in a pre-heated moderate oven (350°F. or Gas Mark 4) for 1$\frac{1}{4}$—1$\frac{1}{2}$ hours, until potatoes are creamy and surface golden. An excellent supper or luncheon dish.

VARIATION

LE GRATIN JURASSIEN
SLICED POTATOES WITH CREAM AND CHEESE
Thickly butter flameproof gratin dish. Slice 1lb. potatoes and arrange in layers with 2 oz. grated Gruyère cheese, tiny dots of butter (1 oz.), and seasoning; finish with cheese. Pour in $\frac{1}{3}$ pint (U.S. $\frac{7}{8}$ cup) double cream and bring slowly almost to simmering point on top of cooker. Cook in centre of a cool oven (300°F. or Gas Mark 2) until tender and golden, 1$\frac{1}{2}$—2 hours.

NOTES ON FRENCH CHEESES

French cheeses repay a little extra care in choosing and storing. Most of them are best eaten when fresh so, if possible, buy from a shop with a fairly rapid turn-over.

SOFT PASTE CHEESES

Including Brie, Camembert, Carré de L'Est, Pont L'Evêque, Livarot, and many others. Although fairly firm and dry when first made these cheeses gradually ripen until soft and creamy in the centre and finally throughout. The right stage to eat them is a matter of personal experiment and taste. When over-ripe they smell unpleasantly strong.

BUYING AND STORING

The more 'give' a cheese has when lightly pressed the sooner it will ripen. Avoid shrunk, discoloured or strong smelling cheeses. Keep in the wrapper or box in a cool airy larder until of desired ripeness, then eat promptly. Do not refrigerate.

WINES TO SERVE

Sound red wines with good bouquet. Gourmets reserve their finest vintage claret for a perfect Brie or Camembert.

SEMI-HARD CHEESES

These include Port-du-Salut, St-Paulin, Tomme au Raisin, Cantal, Comté, Reblochon and so on. They differ from each other in flavour, texture and appearance and for eating raw are best bought freshly in small quantities. Usually cut from a large cheese or bought as pre-packed portions.

BUYING AND STORING

Choose fresh looking cheese. Pre-pack portions should be a neat shape with untorn wrappers. Store in an airy larder, in own wrapper or in greaseproof paper in a polythene bag.

WINES TO SERVE

Light red, or dry fruity white or rosé wines.

BLUE-VEINED CHEESES

These include the famous Roquefort made from ewes milk, and many cows milk cheeses such as Bresse Blue. In texture and flavour they vary from soft, buttery and mildly piquant to the crumbly and pungent. Found in small and large cheeses, or foil wrapped portions.

BUYING AND STORING

Choose fresh looking cheese and avoid discoloured cheese or wrappers. Store lightly wrapped in foil or polythene in a cool larder or least cold area of refrigerator.

WINES TO SERVE

Full bodied red Burgundy wines.

CREAM CHEESES

These include Demi-sel, St. Florentin, Petits Suisse, Fromage Monsieur, Fromage Le Roi, etc. To enjoy the delicate flavour of these cheeses, which contain from 40—75 per cent fat, eat as fresh as possible. Unsalted varieties such as Petits Suisses and Pommel are often served as a dessert with fresh raspberries or strawberries, sugar or thick fresh cream.

BUYING AND STORING

Avoid discoloured or sour smelling cheese. Although very perishable they will keep for several days, covered, in the least cold part of the refrigerator.

WINES TO SERVE

Medium sweet white or rosé wines.

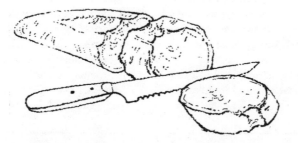

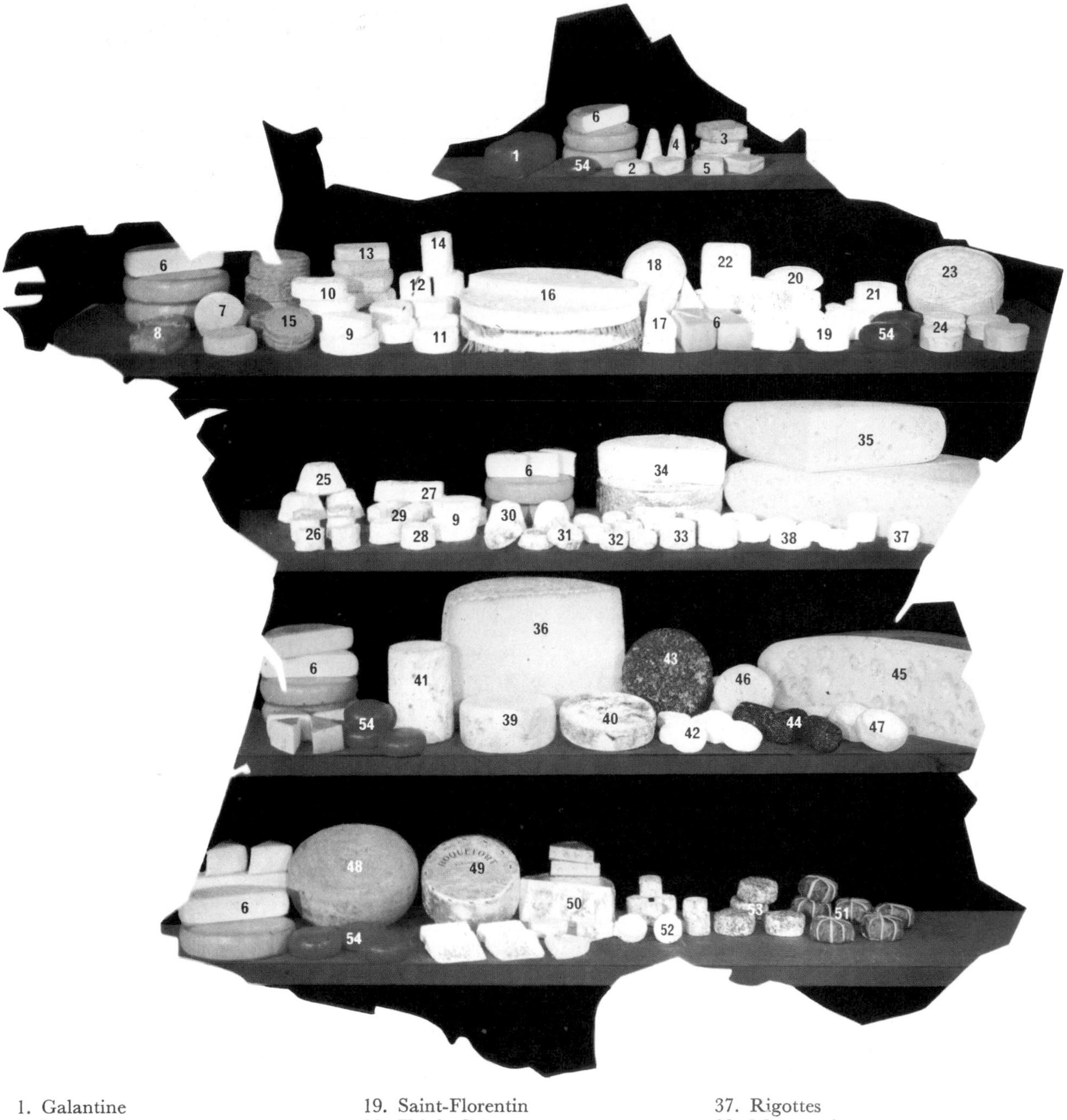

1. Galantine
2. Rollet
3. Maroilles
4. Boulettes d'Avesnes
5. Gris de Lille
6. St-Paulin
7. Petit St-Paulin
8. Nantais dit Cure
9. Camembert
10. Demi-Camembert
11. Triple Crème
12. Triple Crème Aromatise
13. Pont l'Evêque
14. Bondon Neufchatel
15. Livarot
16. Brie
17. Pointe de Brie
18. Coulommiers

19. Saint-Florentin
20. Triple Crème
21. Petit Camembert
22. Carré de l'Est
23. Munster
24. Petit Munster
25. Pyramid (croûte blanche)
26. Chabichou
27. Sainte-Maure
28. Toucy
29. Beauvoir
30. Valençay Levroux
31. Selles-sur-Cher
32. Crottin de Chavignol
33. Bleu de Bresse
34. Saingorlon
35. Comté
36. Cantal

37. Rigottes
38. Maconnais
39. Blue d'Aubergne
40. Saint-Nectaire
41. Fourme d'Ambert
42. Saint-Marcellin
43. Fondu au Raisin
44. Bonde aux Raisins
45. Emmental
46. Reblochon
47. Petit Reblochon
48. Laruns
49. Roquefort
50. Roquefort (portions)
51. Banon
52. Pelardon
53. Poivre d'Ane
54. Croûte Rouge

A selection of French cheeses

Filets de sole Normande (Fillets of sole Normandy style)

It is no good pretending, says Prosper Montagne, for the fact is that this particular method of preparing sole is not expressly Norman. Some hundred years ago this rich and imaginative dish was created by the chef of a then famous Paris restaurant. But in the meantime the town of Rouen has adopted it as its own and certainly Norman chefs excel in making it. The classic version, as indicated by Escoffier, says Prosper Montagne, in addition to the creamy sauce must have a garnish of poached oysters, mussels, button mushrooms, prawns or crayfish, black truffles, goujons or smelts, and croûtons of bread fried in butter or fleurons of puff pastry. Not in fact the sort of dish that can be put together in a few minutes for a ravenous family. However we think you'll find our only slightly simplified version on Page 54 well worth the time and trouble.

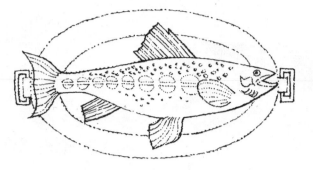

FISH AND SHELLFISH

LES POISSONS ET LES COQUILLES

Innumerable varieties of familiar and unfamiliar fish are caught in the seas around France. When travelling in France make a point of visiting local markets and finding out which restaurants specialise in local fish dishes. It is usually in small back street establishments where the owner is also the chef that colourful and interesting recipes are found. And these, rather than the smoothly sauced soles of the top hotels, are the dishes enjoyed in French homes.

Fascinating and exciting though they are, recipes for Bouillabaisse, La Bourride, Quennelle de Brochet and other Mediterranean or regional specialities have been omitted in favour of those which bring the savour of good French home cooking to our own English fish. And in particular to fish already filleted by the fishmonger or quick freeze process

A good fish dish does not need a wine, but if it is 'an occasion' serve a medium dry white wine (very dry wines are apt to be a little acid with fish), and for a fatty fish like trout, or one cooked in butter, you may find a rosé wine much to your liking.

COQUILLES ST. JACQUES A LA BRETON

ESCALLOPS BRETON STYLE

Preparation time 15 minutes
Cooking time 20–25 minutes
To serve 4

You will need

$3\frac{1}{2}$ oz. butter
about 2 oz. dry white breadcrumbs
1 teaspoon finely grated onion
salt and pepper to taste
8 escallops
$\frac{1}{2}$ lemon
GARNISH
sprigs parsley

Ask the fishmonger for 4 of the *deep* escallop shells; wash and dry them. Melt 3 oz. butter in a saucepan, add enough breadcrumbs to give a moist buttery texture, then stir in the onion and seasoning. Rinse escallops in cold water. Separate the roes (red tongues) and put in a small casserole with a little water and $\frac{1}{2}$ oz. butter; cover. Cut the white part into $\frac{1}{4}$-inch dice. Line deep scallop shells with half the breadcrumbs, lay diced fish on top, sprinkle with lemon juice and cover with remaining crumbs. Bake, uncovered, in a pre-heated moderate oven, (350°F. or Gas Mark 4), for about 20—25 minutes until fish cooked and crumbs crisp. Cook roes in casserole alongside.

Serve in the shell, each garnished with 2 roes and a sprig of parsley.

Fillets of sole with grapes

FILETS DE POISSON
A LA MEUNIÈRE

FISH FILLETS
MILLERS WIFE STYLE

Preparation time 10 minutes
Cooking time 5–6 minutes
To serve 4

You will need

4 large fillets plaice *or* sole
little well seasoned flour
2—3 oz. unsalted *or* clarified butter
1 tablespoon oil
1 tablespoon lemon juice
1 tablespoon chopped fresh parsley

Remove dark skin, then wipe and dry fish fillets. Coat evenly with seasoned flour. Heat enough butter and oil in a large frying pan to give ⅛-inch depth. When foaming put in the fillets, flat, and skinned side uppermost. Cook over low heat until golden brown then turn carefully and cook other side, about 2—3 minutes each side. Remove to a very hot dish and sprinkle with lemon juice and parsley. Wipe out pan, put in 1 oz. fresh butter and heat until beginning to turn brown and smell 'nutty'. Immediately pour over fish and rush to table still sizzling hot.

VARIATION

SOLE MEUNIÈRE AUX RAISINS
FILLETS OF SOLE WITH GRAPES

Peel and pip 6 oz. muscat *or* white grapes. Sprinkle with lemon juice and leave in a warm place to

heat gently. Scatter over cooked fish just before serving.

TRUITES AUX AMANDES
TROUT WITH ALMONDS

Preparation time 10 minutes
Cooking time 12–15 minutes
To serve 4

You will need

4 fresh trout, 4–5 oz. each*
little seasoned flour
2 oz. unsalted butter
juice half lemon
1½ oz. flaked blanched almonds
GARNISH
lemon slices

* Portions of halibut *or* brill are good cooked in the same way.

Ask the fishmonger to clean the trout through the gills but leave the heads on. Dry the fish and roll in seasoned flour. Melt 1½ oz. butter in a heavy frying pan large enough to hold the fish flat. When hot put in the fish and fry over *low* heat for about 5 minutes each side, until cooked, golden and crisp. Watch they do not stick to the pan whilst

Trout with almonds

cooking. Lift onto a hot serving dish and sprinkle with lemon juice. Add remaining butter to pan and fry almonds until golden brown, stirring frequently. Spoon over trout and serve immediately, garnished with slices of lemon.

MACKEREL EN PAPILLOTES

MACKEREL IN PAPER BAGS

Preparation time 10 minutes
Cooking time about 30 minutes
To serve 4

You will need

4 fresh small mackerel
oil
2 oz. butter, softened
2 heaped tablespoons chopped fresh herbs
   (parsley, chives, fennel)
1 tablespoon drained capers, chopped
salt and ground black pepper
2 teaspoons lemon juice

Ask the fishmonger to clean the mackerel but to leave the heads on.
Brush with oil and grill or fry quickly to stiffen and colour the skin but not to cook through. Cut 4 ovals of foil or greaseproof paper, 2-inches longer than the fish, and brush with oil. Mix together the softened butter, chopped fresh herbs, capers,

Mackerel in paper bags

seasoning and lemon juice and stuff the mackerel. Place in the centre of the pieces of foil or greaseproof paper and fold over the edges securely making a *loose* parcel from which juices cannot escape. Bake in a fireproof dish in a preheated oven (350°F. or Gas Mark 4), for 20—25 minutes. Serve from the baking dish, cutting the paper and transferring fish and buttery juices to hot plates, at the table.

MULLET A LA NIÇOISE

COLD MULLET NICE STYLE

Preparation time 10 minutes
Cooking time 15 minutes plus 2 hours
                cooling
To serve 4

You will need

4 small red mullet
salt and pepper
olive oil for frying
SAUCE
2 shallots, finely chopped
1 clove garlic, crushed
1 tablespoon olive oil
1 lb. ripe tomatoes, peeled
salt and pepper
GARNISH
8 anchovy fillets
some stoned green olives

Ask the fishmonger to gut and scale the fish but leave the heads on. Season inside with salt and pepper. Heat a little oil in a heavy frying pan and fry the fish over low heat until cooked and golden, about 5—7 minutes each side.

TO MAKE THE SAUCE:

Fry shallots and garlic in the oil over *low* heat, about 5 minutes. Peel and remove seeds from tomatoes. Chop and add to the shallots and garlic. Cook steadily, stirring frequently, until reduced to a thick sauce consistency; season to taste. Arrange fish in a shallow serving dish, pour the hot sauce over and leave to become cold. Cut anchovy fillets into thin strips and arrange in criss-cross pattern over the fish. Garnish with olives.

POISSON
AU COURT – BOUILLON

FISH POACHED IN STOCK

Fish is never boiled in water in France. A special stock known as a court-bouillon, is prepared as follows: Into a large saucepan put 3 pints (U.S. 7½ cups) water, 1 sliced onion and carrot, 3—4 parsley stalks, 1 level tablespoon salt, 6 peppercorns and either 6 tablespoons white wine *or* 3 tablespoons vinegar. Cover and simmer for 30 minutes. Allow to cool then put in the fish and poach (the water should just tremble not bubble) for 10—12 minutes per lb.

TO SERVE HOT:

Drain fish thoroughly and serve with a rich sauce such as Hollandaise, Beurre Blanc, Soubise or Béarnaise (see pages 120, 121).

TO SERVE COLD:

Allow fish to cool in the stock, then drain and serve with a mayonnaise base sauce (see page 119) *or* a Tomato Coulis (see page 122).

Fish grilled over fennel

pieces of skate into the pan and simmer gently for 12—15 minutes. Drain fish, cut off extreme bony fringe, and arrange on a *hot* dish. Heat butter gently in small frying pan until it turns nut brown then immediately pour over fish. Heat wine vinegar in the same pan until slightly reduced. Sprinkle capers (if used) and parsley over fish then pour vinegar over and serve quickly, while sizzling hot.

RAIE AU BEURRE NOIR

SKATE WITH 'BLACK BUTTER'

Preparation time 10 minutes
Cooking time   20 minutes
To serve   4

You will need

4 portions skate, 6–8 oz. each, skinned
COURT BOUILLON
2 pints (U.S. 5 cups) water
1 onion, sliced
2 tablespoons vinegar
2 level teaspoons salt
6 peppercorns
BEURRE NOIR
2 oz. butter
2 tablespoons wine vinegar
1 tablespoon drained capers (optional)
2 teaspoons chopped parsley

In a wide saucepan boil the water, onion, vinegar, salt and peppercorns for 5 minutes. Lower the

LIMANDES A LA BRETONNE

LEMON SOLE BRITTANY STYLE

Preparation time 15 minutes
Cooking time   10 minutes
To serve   4

You will need

4 lemon soles *or* dabs, whole
2 oz. well seasoned flour
about 4 oz. butter
1 tablespoon oil
1 tablespoon finely chopped shallot *or* onion
2 oz. shelled shrimps *or* small prawns
1 level tablespoon capers
1 tablespoon chopped herbs (parsley, chives and chervil)
juice 1 lemon

Trim fish, remove heads and wipe dry. Coat with seasoned flour. Heat 2 oz. butter and oil in a large frying pan and when hot fry fish, one or two at a time, about 4—5 minutes on each side. Arrange on a hot dish. Meanwhile melt 1½ oz. butter in a small frying pan, fry the shallot *or* onion gently until soft, then add shrimps *or* prawns, capers, herbs and lemon juice. Heat gently and pour over the fish

---

FILETS DE POISSONS GRATINÉE AU FOUR

FISH FILLETS BROWNED IN THE OVEN

Preparation time 15 minutes
Cooking time   15–25 minutes
To serve   4

You will need

2 oz. butter
1 tablespoon finely chopped onion
4 oz. mushrooms, finely chopped
¼ pint (U.S. ⅝ cup) dry white wine
1¼ lb. white fish fillets
salt and pepper
2 heaped tablespoons fresh white breadcrumbs
1 tablespoon chopped parsley

Melt 1 oz. butter and fry onion over *low* heat until soft but not coloured. Add mushrooms and cook for 1 minute, add wine and boil rapidly for another minute. Lay fish fillets in a buttered shallow oven-proof dish, season, and pour wine mixture over them. Sprinkle evenly with breadcrumbs and dot with remaining butter. Cook near top of pre-heated oven (425°F. or Gas Mark 7), for thin fillets, but (400°F. or Gas Mark 6) for thick fillets, for 15—20 minutes until fish just cooked and crumbs golden and crisp. Sprinkle with parsley, and serve hot, in the same dish.

GRILLADE AU FENOUIL

FISH GRILLED OVER FENNEL

Preparation time 5 minutes
Cooking time   15–20 minutes
To serve   depends on size of fish

You will need

suitable fish*
salt and pepper
olive oil
dried fennel stalks
* red mullet, sea bass *or* small John Dory

Clean fish and make several incisions on each side. Season and brush with olive oil. Grill for about 5 minutes on each side. Spread fennel on a large *flameproof* dish and over it stand a high legged metal grid. Lay partially cooked fish on grid. Set fennel alight with matches (in smart restaurants this is done with brandy) and let fish continue cooking over fennel for another several minutes on each side, according to thickness of fish. It should have long enough to become pleasantly perfumed with fennel smoke.

Note

Fennel is easily grown (see page 107). The feathery foliage makes a delightful garnish as well as an addition to sauces, and the stalks can be hung up and dried.

POISSONS A LA PROVENÇALE

WHITE FISH PROVENÇAL STYLE

Preparation time 15 minutes
Cooking time   10–12 minutes
To serve   4

You will need

1½ lb. fillet of cod, haddock *or* hake
1 oz. seasoned flour
oil for frying
1 medium-sized onion, finely sliced
1 clove garlic, crushed
¾ lb. tomatoes, peeled, seeded and sliced
1 level teaspoon chopped fresh herbs (parsley, chives and chervil)
salt and pepper to taste
black olives for garnish (optional)

Cut fish into 2-inch squares then roll in seasoned flour. In a frying pan heat a little oil, then fry fish quickly until golden brown on both sides, approximately 8 minutes. Drain, arrange in a shallow serving dish and keep hot. Strain off surplus oil leaving one good tablespoonful in the pan. Fry onion until tender, add the garlic, tomato and herbs. Toss quickly over brisk heat for 2—3 minutes. Season and add olives (if used). Pour over the fish.

FILETS DE SOLE NORMANDE

FILLETS OF SOLE NORMANDY STYLE

(Illustrated in colour on page 48)
Preparation time 15 minutes
Cooking time 25–30 minutes
To serve 4

You will need

FISH
8 fillets sole
salt and pepper
2 level tablespoons chopped shallot *or* onion
2 sprigs parsley and half bay leaf
½ pint (U.S. 1¼ cups) dry white wine
SAUCE
1½ oz. butter
1½ oz. flour
2 egg yolks
¼ pint (U.S. ⅝ cup) double cream
few drops lemon juice
GARNISH
8 prawns *or* 4 crayfish, cooked
2 pints (U.S. 5 cups) mussels
2 truffles (optional)
8 button mushrooms
8 crescents of fried bread *or* baked puff pastry

One of the great classic dishes. Season the fillets, roll up, and arrange in buttered shallow ovenproof dish with the shallot *or* onion, herbs and wine. Cover with buttered greaseproof paper. Poach in a pre-heated moderate oven (375°F. or Gas Mark 5), until cooked, about 15—20 minutes. Meanwhile wash mussels thoroughly, discard any that fail to shut tightly when tapped, and scrape off beards. Put into a large pan, cover, and shake over sharp heat until shells open, about 5 minutes. Remove mussels from shells; strain and retain liquor from pan. Wipe mushrooms and cook 'à blanc' as described on page 98. Strain and reserve liquor. Now make the rich sauce Normande. Melt butter in a saucepan, stir in flour and cook gently, stirring, for 2 minutes. Strain cooking liquor from fish into a measure, add mussel and mushroom liquor to make up to ¾ pint (U.S. 3⅞cups). Add to roux, whisking with wire whisk until sauce is smooth and boiling; simmer 5 minutes. Meanwhile beat egg yolks and cream together, gradually stir in about one-third of the sauce, then return all to rest of sauce and heat gently *without boiling*, stirring all the time. Check seasoning and add a few drops of lemon juice.

Arrange drained fish in clean hot dish with mussels and mushrooms. Coat with the sauce and garnish with the prawns *or* crayfish, pieces of truffle (if used), and crescents of fried bread or pastry.

Note

The original classic recipe includes 8 poached oysters as well as the mussels.

BRANDADE DE MORUE

CREAMED SALT COD

Preparation time overnight
Cooking time 30–40 minutes
To serve 3–4

You will need

1 lb. salt codfish
1 small clove garlic, crushed
¼ pint (U.S. ⅝ cup) olive oil
1 level tablespoon cornflour
¼ pint (U.S. ⅝ cup) milk
pepper to taste
about 1 tablespoon lemon juice
GARNISH
triangles of fried bread

Soak fish overnight in cold water. Drain, cover with fresh water and bring *slowly* to the boil. Simmer gently for 10 minutes. Drain, and remove all bones and skin. Flake fish and put with garlic

Creamed salt cod

and 2 tablespoons oil into a heavy casserole standing on an asbestos mat over *low* heat. Beat vigorously with a wooden spoon. Mix cornflour smoothly with a little of the milk, bring rest of milk to boil and stir in cornflour; simmer for 2 minutes, stirring. Warm remainder of the oil. Add to the fish alternately a spoonful of oil and cornflour sauce (both warm but *not* hot) beating vigorously all the time. The result should be a soft creamy mixture. Season to taste with pepper and lemon juice. Pile into a warm serving dish and garnish with triangles of fried bread.

HOMARD A LA CRÈME

LOBSTER WITH CREAM SAUCE

Preparation time 10 minutes
Cooking time about 12 minutes
To serve 2

You will need

1 freshly cooked lobster, about 1 lb.
2 oz. butter
2 oz. button mushrooms, sliced
2 tablespoons brandy
2 tablespoons dry Madeira *or* sherry
salt and cayenne pepper
¼ pint (U.S. ⅝ cup) double cream

Twist off the claws and with a large sharp knife split the lobster lengthwise down the back. Lay flat the two halves cut side uppermost and discard the stomach bag (from the head) and the black intestinal cord. Remove the tail and claw meat and cut into slant-wise slices.
Melt 1 oz. butter in a saucepan and over low heat cook the mushrooms for 1—2 minutes, remove and keep warm. Add the remaining butter and the lobster to the same pan, cover and heat gently for several minutes. Pour the brandy into a heated ladle, light with a match and pour flaming over the lobster. When the flames die, add Madeira *or* sherry, a little salt and one shake cayenne. Heat for a minute then add cream and cook gently, stirring frequently, until cream thickens. Return mushrooms to pan and spoon mixture into lobster shells. Serve hot.

COURONNE DE RIZ AUX CREVETTES

CREAMED PRAWNS IN RICE RING

Preparation time 20 minutes
Cooking time 30 minutes
To serve 4

RICE RING
2 oz. butter
1 oz. finely chopped onion
8 oz. rice
1 pint (U.S. 2½ cups) boiling fish *or* chicken stock
CREAMED PRAWNS
1 tablespoon finely chopped shallots *or* onion
2 oz. butter
6–8 oz. shelled prawns
2 tablespoons dry white wine, white vermouth, *or* sherry
1 oz. flour
scant ½ pint (U.S. 1¼ cups) boiling milk
2 tablespoons double cream
1 oz. Gruyère cheese grated
salt and pepper
GARNISH
8 prawns in shell (optional)

Heat butter in flameproof casserole and cook onions until soft. Add rice and stir until translucent. Pour in boiling stock, season if necessary, and bring to the boil. Cover tightly, transfer to a pre-heated moderate oven (350°F. or Gas Mark 4), for 20 minutes or until liquid completely absorbed. Fluff rice with fork and pack into buttered 2-pint ring mould. Smooth surface, cover and return to warm oven for 10 minutes. While rice is cooking make filling as follows. Fry shallot *or* onion very gently in 1 oz. melted butter then stir in prawns. Add wine *or* sherry and heat until almost evaporated. In separate saucepan melt remaining 1 oz. butter, add flour, and cook for 2 minutes. Whisk in the milk and boil, stirring, for 1 minute. Stir in the cream, prawn mixture and cheese, season and heat gently without boiling.
Unmould rice ring onto hot dish and fill centre with creamed prawns. Garnish with whole prawns and serve hot.

MOULES MARINIÈRES

MUSSELS SAILOR STYLE

Preparation time 15 minutes
Cooking time 7–8 minutes
To serve 3

You will need

4 pints (U.S. 10 cups) fresh mussels
2 shallots, chopped
4 stalks parsley
sprig thyme
ground black pepper
⅓ pint (U.S. ⅞ cup) dry white wine
1 oz. butter
little chopped parsley

Scrape and clean mussels in several changes of cold water, discarding any that do not shut tightly. Put into a wide pan with shallots, herbs, pepper and wine. Cover pan and cook over sharp heat for 5—6 minutes, shaking pan now and then. Remove mussels as soon as open, discarding one half of each shell. Arrange mussels in remaining shells in warm soup plates. Strain liquid through muslin, return to pan with butter and boil rapidly till reduced by half. Pour over mussels, and sprinkle with chopped parsley. Serve at once with crusty French bread, creamy butter and dry white wine or cider.

VARIATION

MOULES A LA CRÈME
MUSSELS WITH CREAM

Add ¼ pint (U.S. ⅝ cup) double cream instead of butter to the reduced mussel liquor and boil rapidly for several minutes before pouring over mussels.

SOUPE AUX MOULES

MUSSELS WITH TOMATO

(Illustrated in colour opposite)
Preparation time 20 minutes
Cooking time 10 minutes
To serve 2

You will need

3 pints (U.S. 7½ cups) small fresh mussels
1 oz. butter
3 oz. onion, chopped
8 oz. ripe tomatoes
6 tablespoons dry white wine
ground black pepper
fresh chopped parsley

Scrub and scrape the mussels in several changes of cold water, discarding any that fail to shut tightly.
Melt the butter in a wide pan and over a low heat fry the chopped onion for 5 minutes or until soft and golden. Skin and chop the tomatoes and add with the wine to the onions. Allow to boil for a minute then put in the prepared mussels. Cover, and cook over quick heat, shaking the pan from time to time, until the mussels open, about 5 minutes.
Discard the shells as they open, and serve the mussels immediately with the cooking liquor strained over them.
Season to taste with a little ground black pepper and garnish with a little fresh chopped parsley.
Serve with crusty French bread and creamy butter.

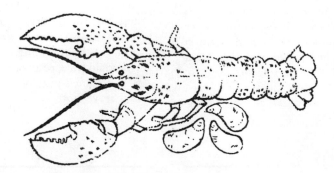

Soupe aux moules (Mussels with tomato)

Carré de porc rôti (Roast rolled loin of pork)

A succulent joint of rolled pork or lamb fragrant with the scent of herbs and garlic takes one, if only in the mind's eye, to some sunny country inn among the hillsides of Provence.

There you will tuck into a thick slice of roast meat accompanied by a mousseline of potatoes over which has been poured some of the richly aromatic juices from the roast.

Aromatic is the word to describe the herbs that flourish in Provence — marjoram, rosemary, wild thyme, fennel, bay — all are more assertive than similar varieties grown in more northerly climates.

If you want to add a touch of nostalgia to many a winter dish, bring home some herbs dried on the stalk in the Mediterranean sun.

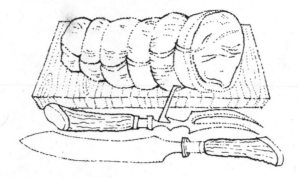

MEATS

LES VIANDES

The French are equally adept at cooking the cheaper cuts of meat as well as prime cuts. The former are the basis of much traditional household cookery and many recipes for wine stews and braises are given in the Casserole chapter. Pot-au-feu comes in the Soup section.

This chapter deals mainly with prime cuts and steaks but includes offal and a few recipes using cheaper cuts. Good butchering is an art in France and the methods of cutting meat are quite different from those in England. Joints for roasting and braising are invariably boned and rolled making them easy to carve. Lean braising cuts are larded through the centre with strips of pork fat which keeps them moist from within during cooking, making otherwise dry meat deliciously succulent. Lean roasting joints are usually tied round with a thin slice of fat which makes basting unnecessary. By our standards the French like their meat, especially beef and lamb, undercooked. But this is a matter of personal preference.

Roast meats and steaks are served with the natural juices which run from the meat or with a herb flavoured butter. One vegetable usually accompanies a meat dish, and a salad is often served separately.

BIFTECKS

BEEFSTEAKS

To be tender and of good flavour a beef steak must always be cut from well hung meat. On this both French and British butchers are agreed, although methods of jointing meat are quite different. The following are the generally accepted descriptions of various French steak cuts.

BIFTECK
A general term given to a lean boneless steak from any reasonably tender part of the beef.

ENTRECÔTE
A rib steak.

ROMSTECK OR RUMPSTECK
A steak cut from the rump.

CHÂTEAUBRIAND
A very thick cut from centre of fillet. Usually grilled, and enough for 2 people.

FILET
A steak from $\frac{3}{4}$-1-inch thick cut from centre of fillet.

TOURNEDOS
Thick round fillet or rump steaks about 3-inches in diameter, encircled with pork fat.

MINUTE
A very thin steak cut from the entrecôte or rump. It is cooked very quickly.

Note
A plain grilled steak is usually garnished with watercress, topped with plain or herb butter (Maître d'hôtel or Beurre d'escargots, see page 118) and served with French fried or purée potatoes.

BIFTECK SAUTÉ MARCHAND DE VINS

BEEFSTEAK WITH WINE SAUCE

Preparation time 5 minutes
Cooking time 10 minutes
To serve 4

You will need

4 rump *or* entrecôte steaks, ¾–1-inch thick
2 oz. butter
1 tablespoon olive oil
salt and ground black pepper
¼ pint (U.S. ⅝ cup) red wine *or* vermouth

Trim steaks and pat dry. Heat 1 oz. butter and the oil in a heavy frying pan and fry steaks over medium heat for 3—4 minutes each side. When small beads of red juice begin to ooze from surface the steak is cooked medium rare (à point). Remove steaks, season and keep warm. Pour off any surplus or burnt fat. Add wine *or* vermouth to pan and boil furiously, scraping up coagulated juices with a wooden spoon, until reduced to about 4 tablespoons. Off the heat stir in remaining butter. Pour sauce over steaks and serve.

TOURNEDOS HENRI IV

TOURNEDOS STEAKS WITH BÉARNAISE SAUCE

Preparation time 20 minutes
Cooking time 20 minutes, including sauce
To serve 4

1½ lb. slice tender rump *or* fillet steak,
 1½-inches thick
strips of back pork fat for larding
1 recipe Béarnaise sauce (see page 120)
3-inch round bread croûtons fried in butter
½ oz. butter
1 dessertspoon oil
salt and pepper
GARNISH
cooked potato chips
sprigs watercress

Tournedos
Cutting the tournedos

Using a 3-inch round cutter as a guide cut 4 circles of meat from the slice. Cut strips of pork fat the same depth as the meat and tie around outside of each steak. (Many butchers will prepare the Tournedos for you).
When ready to cook make the Béarnaise sauce and keep warm (not hot) by standing the pan in a water bath.
Fry the croûtons of bread until crisp and golden and arrange on a flat serving dish. Heat the butter oil in a heavy frying pan and when hot fry the steaks for 3—4 minutes on each side.
Season and arrange each on a croûton, removing the larding fat or not as you wish.
Pipe or spoon a little Béarnaise sauce around each Tournedos and serve the rest separately.
Pile hot potato chips in the centre of dish and garnish with sprigs of watercress.

VARIATION
TOURNEDOS ROSSINI

Prepare and cook the tournedos steaks as above. Remove the string and arrange on croûtons of fried bread. Place a thin slice of foie gras on top of each tournedos and place under a hot grill for a minute to warm and soften the foie gras. Pour off the excess fat from frying pan, add 4 tablespoons Madeira wine and boil until reduced by half. Add 2 tablespoons stock and 1—2 oz. chopped black truffles.
Off the heat stir in 1 oz. butter. Spoon a little sauce over each steak and garnish with fried potatoes.

Tournedos
Tying a strip of back pork fat around the tournedos

Tournedos
The finished dish

BIFTECK SAUTÉ AU BEURRE
STEAK SAUTÉD IN BUTTER

Preparation time 5 minutes
Cooking time 8–10 minutes
To serve 4

You will need

4 tender steaks, about 1-inch thick
1 oz. butter
1 dessertspoon olive oil
salt and pepper
¼ pint (U.S. ⅝ cup) stock *or* red *or* white wine
1 oz. softened butter*

GARNISH
potato chips
sprigs watercress

* Better still, Maître d'hôtel or Garlic butter (see page 118).

Trim steaks and dry thoroughly. Heat the butter and oil in large frying pan and when hot sauté steaks for 3—4 minutes on each side. The steak will be cooked to medium rare (à point) when tiny 'beads' of juice appear on the surface. Remove steaks, season with salt and pepper and keep hot. Pour fat out of pan. Add stock *or* wine, and with wooden spoon stir and scrape juices from bottom of pan whilst boiling rapidly until liquid is reduced to half. Off the heat stir in softened butter which will slightly thicken the juices. Pour a spoonful or so over each steak and serve garnished with potato chips and watercress. Serve a green salad separately.

BIFTECK SAUTÉ BERCY
STEAKS WITH SHALLOT AND BUTTER SAUCE

Preparation time 10 minutes
Cooking time 10 minutes
To serve 4

You will need

4 rump or fillet steaks, ¾-inch thick
3 oz. butter
1 tablespoon oil
salt and ground black pepper
2 oz. finely chopped shallot *or* spring onion
¼ pint dry white wine
1 heaped tablespoon chopped fresh parsley

GARNISH
watercress

Beat steaks to flatten slightly and wipe dry. Heat 1 oz. butter and the oil in a heavy frying pan and fry steaks fairly briskly for 3—4 minutes each side. Season and transfer to a hot serving dish. Add ½ oz. butter and the shallots *or* spring onion to the frying pan and cook gently for 2 minutes. Add wine, stir and scrape meat juices from the bottom of pan, then boil rapidly until well reduced and syrupy. Off the heat stir in remaining butter, ½ oz. at a time, to enrich and thicken sauce. Check seasoning, add parsley and spoon over steaks. Garnish with watercress and serve with creamed potatoes or miniature chips.

Roast beef with vegetables

ROTI DE BOEUF JARDINIÈRE

ROAST BEEF WITH VEGETABLES

Preparation time 20 minutes
Cooking time 1½ hours
To serve 9–10 portions

You will need

3 lb. eye of sirloin boned and rolled
salt and pepper
little olive oil
¼ pint (U.S. ⅝ cup) dry red *or* white wine,
  or beef stock
GARNISH
Pomme Parisienne (see page 100)
haricots verts
new carrots

This is a favourite way of serving roast beef in France. Any choice young vegetables in season can be arranged around the meat.
Pre-heat oven to (425°F. or Gas Mark 7). Rub the meat with salt and pepper and brush the cut surfaces with olive oil. Stand on a rack in a roasting tin and cook in centre of oven for 15 minutes. Reduce heat to (350°F. or Gas Mark 4) and continue cooking for 1¼ hours.
Meanwhile prepare the Pomme Parisienne and the other vegetable garnishes.
Arrange the meat on along dish with the vegetables grouped around it. Skim surplus fat from roasting tin and add the red *or* white wine, *or* beef stock. Stir and boil, scraping up coagulated juices from bottom of tin.

Season if necessary and pour into hot gravy boat to serve with the meat.

FILET DE BOEUF EN CROUTE

FILLET OF BEEF IN PASTRY

Preparation time 20 minutes
Cooking time about 45 minutes
To serve 6

You will need

2 lb. fillet of beef
2 oz. butter
1 tablespoon olive oil
1 small onion, finely chopped
4 oz. button mushrooms, sliced
4 tablespoons red wine
salt and ground black pepper
8 oz. (made-up weight) puff *or* flaky pastry
beaten egg for glazing

Trim the fillet of beef removing any fat or tissue. Heat 1 oz. of the butter and the oil in a frying pan and brown meat quickly on all sides. Remove, season, leave to get cold. Fry the prepared onion in same pan and when soft add the remaining butter and the mushrooms; cook gently 2—3 minutes. Add the wine and salt and ground black pepper and bubble briskly until wine reduced by half. Leave till cold. (All this can be done in advance).
Pre-heat oven to (425°F. or Gas Mark 7). Roll pastry *thinly* into a rectangle large enough to envelop meat and overlap generously; damp the edges. Place the meat on pastry, spoon the mushroom mixture over.
Fold the pastry over the meat and turn the ends upwards to prevent the escape of juices. Brush with egg and bake for 15 minutes, then reduce heat to (375°F. or Gas Mark 5) and cook another 30—40 minutes depending on thickness of fillet.
The pastry should be golden and crisp and the meat juicy and 'rare'.
This dish is excellent hot or cold.

BIFTECK AU POIVRE

PEPPER STEAKS

Preparation time   10 minutes
Cooking time   10 minutes
To serve   4

You will need

4 thin rump steaks, ¼-inch thick
1 oz. white peppercorns
2 oz. butter
1 dessertspoon oil
salt
scant ¼ pint (U.S. ⅝ cup) beef stock
2–3 tablespoons brandy
GARNISH
watercress

Beat steaks and wipe dry. Crush peppercorns (use a heavy weight or pestle and mortar) and press into meat on both sides. Cover and leave for at least 30 minutes. Heat 1 oz. butter and the oil in a heavy pan and fry steaks for 2 minutes each side; sprinkle with salt, remove to serving dish and keep warm. Add stock and brandy to the pan, stirring and scraping juices from the bottom, and boil rapidly for 2—3 minutes. Off the heat stir in remaining butter, ½ oz. at a time. Spoon sauce over steaks and garnish with watercress. Serve with sauté *or* creamed potatoes.

Cook-it-yourself steak Burgundy style

A popular cook-it-yourself party dish. Trim meat and cut into ¾-inch cubes. Put each guest's portion on a separate plate, plus a fork for eating and a long handled cooking fork or a kebab type skewer with insulated handles. Stand a fondue pan like the one in the photograph (or a copper saucepan on a trivet) over a spirit stove in centre of the table, and one third fill with oil. Heat gently to 375°F. (a cube of firm bread will turn golden in less than a minute) and maintain at this heat. Guests spear meat on to cooking fork, a cube at a time, and cook in the oil for 1—2 minutes according to taste. Remove meat from cooking fork and season to taste. Eat with chosen accompaniments.

FONDUE BOURGUIGNONNE

COOK-IT-YOURSELF STEAK BURGUNDY STYLE

Preparation time   varies according to
                     accompaniments
Cooking time   1–2 minutes
To serve   any number

You will need

6 oz. lean beef fillet per person
olive *or* corn oil for frying
salt and ground black pepper
ACCOMPANIMENTS
hot French bread, and butter
green *or* chicory salad
raw celery; pickled gherkins; olives
several sauces e. g. Tartare, Vinaigrette,
    Béarnaise (see pages 109, 119, 120)

BIFTECK HACHÉ A LA LYONNAISE

MINCED BEEF CAKES LYON STYLE

Fry 2 oz. chopped onion *slowly* in 1 tablespoon olive oil, about 10 minutes. Put into mixing bowl, add 1 lb. minced beef, seasoning and 1 egg; mix thoroughly. Form into 4 round cakes about ¾-inch thick, and coat with a little flour. Heat 1 tablespoon olive oil and fry cakes for 3—4 minutes on each side. Dish and keep hot. Add ¼ pint (U.S. ⅝ cup.) beef stock *or* dry wine and boil rapidly until well reduced and syrupy. Off heat stir in 1 oz. softened butter and spoon the sauce over the meat.

COTELETTES DE PORC AUX HERBES

PORK CHOPS WITH HERBS

Preparation time 10 minutes plus time to
                           marinate
Cooking time   40 minutes
To serve   3

You will need

3 pork chops, without rind
1 large cut clove garlic
salt and ground black pepper
3 bay leaves
3 sprigs fresh *or* dried thyme
3 tablespoons olive oil

Several hours before cooking rub the pork chops
with the cut garlic and with salt and pepper.
Spread the herbs in a shallow flameproof dish
large enough to take the chops in a single layer.
Arrange the meat on top and spoon the olive oil
over them. Leave to marinate for several hours.
To cook, pre-heat grill and brown chops quickly
on each side, then cover dish and transfer to a
pre-heated very moderate oven (325°F. or Gas
Mark 3), for 30—40 minutes. Serve in the same
dish having first drained off the fat. A green *or*
tomato salad and creamed *or* new potatoes go well
with this dish.

CARRÉ DU PORC ROTI

ROAST ROLLED LOIN OF PORK

(Illustrated in colour on page 58)
Preparation time 10 minutes
Cooking time   1¾ hours
To serve   8–9 portions

You will need

3 lb. boned loin of pork with rind removed
salt and ground black pepper
2 cloves garlic, peeled and sliced (optional)
sprigs fresh rosemary (optional)
¼ pint (U.S. ⅝ cup) white wine ⎫
¼ pint (U.S. ⅝ cup) water   ⎬ *or* all water
GARNISH (optional) ⎭
braised celery
stewed sweet red peppers

Ask butcher to give you the rind and bones from
the meat. Spread meat flat, season with salt and
pepper, form into a roll and tie in several places.
Place fat side up in a roasting dish with garlic and
2 sprigs rosemary (if used), beneath. Arrange
bones and cut up rind around meat. Cook in a pre-
heated hot oven (400°F. or Gas Mark 6), for
30 minutes. Lower heat to (350°F. or Gas Mark 4),
and pour wine and water *or* water around meat.
Cover with a lid or foil (this makes the meat more
succulent) and continue cooking for another 1¼
hours. Dish meat having first removed the strings.
Strain cooking liquor into a small pan, skim off
surplus fat, and reduce if necessary by rapid boiling.
Check seasoning and pour into gravy boat. Garnish
meat with fresh sprigs of rosemary and if liked
with braised celery and stewed sweet red peppers.

Note

The spiky herb rosemary is much used for flavouring pork and lamb in the South of France. It has
a strong flavour and if used take care no spikes are
left in the meat.

COTELETTES DE PORC A LA CHARCUTERIE

PORK CHOPS PORK-BUTCHERS STYLE

Preparation time 5 minutes, excluding sauce
Cooking time   30 minutes
To serve   4

You will need

1 recipe Sauce Piquante (see page 121)
4 pork chops
½ oz. lard *or* butter
1 small onion, finely chopped
2 tablespoons wine vinegar
seasoning to taste

Prepare the sauce in advance. Fry chops slowly in
melted fat, turning once, until cooked through,
about 20 minutes. Season and keep hot. Drain off
all but 1 tablespoon of fat from the frying pan;
add onion and fry gently until soft and golden. Add
vinegar and cook briskly until almost evaporated,
then add Sauce Piquante and season to taste. Boil
for a minute or so and pour over the chops.

PIEDS DE PORC SAINTE MÉNÉHOULD

GRILLED PIGS TROTTERS

Preparation time 15 minutes
Cooking time 3½ hours
To serve 4

You will need

4 large plump pigs trotters
1 onion stuck with a clove
1 carrot, cleaned
1 leek, cleaned
1 bay leaf
1 sprig thyme
3 peppercorns
salt
white breadcrumbs
melted pork fat *or* butter

Ask butcher to split trotters lengthwise. Wash them well and wind a strip of muslin around each to keep it in shape. Put into a pan, cover with cold water and add the vegetables, herbs, peppercorns and salt. Cover and simmer for 3 hours, or until tender. Drain. Remove muslin and discard visible bones. Place trotters side by side in grill pan, cut side uppermost. Sprinkle with breadcrumbs and drizzle a tablespoon of melted fat over each. Grill slowly and serve with Sauce Tartare (see page 119) *or* French mustard.

COTELETTES DE PORC AUX PRUNEAUX

PORK CUTLETS WITH PRUNES

Preparation time 15 minutes plus overnight soaking
Cooking time 45 minutes
To serve 4

You will need

12 large prunes
½ bottle dry white wine
4 large pork chops
seasoned flour
1 oz. butter
1 tablespoon oil
1 level tablespoon redcurrant jelly
4 tablespoons double cream

Soak prunes overnight in ½ pint (U.S. 1¼ cups) of the wine. Next day simmer gently until tender, about 30 minutes. Bone the chops, remove excess fat and flatten slightly. Coat with seasoned flour. Heat butter and oil in a sauté pan and fry meat gently for 5 minutes each side; add remaining wine, cover and simmer until tender, about 20 minutes. Arrange meat down centre of oval serving dish; keep hot. Strain wine from prunes into sauté pan, stir and scrape juices from bottom of pan then boil rapidly until reduced by half. Add the jelly and when dissolved stir in the cream. Boil until thick then pour over meat. Arrange warm prunes on either side and serve hot.

TRANCHE DE JAMBON ROSE-MARIE

HAM SLICES IN CREAM SAUCE

Preparation time 10 minutes
Cooking time about 20 minutes
To serve 4–5

You will need

4–5 slices cooked ham, ¼-inch thick
1 oz. butter
1 dessertspoon oil
1 tablespoon shallots *or* spring onions, finely chopped
1 level tablespoon flour
¼ pint (U.S. ⅝ cup) ham *or* chicken stock
4 tablespoons Madeira *or* sweet white wine
1 teaspoon tomato purée
ground black pepper
¼ pint (U.S. ⅝ cup) double cream

Trim excess fat from ham; pat dry. Heat butter and oil in large frying pan and fry ham slices a few at a time until lightly browned; set aside. Leave 1 tablespoon of fat in pan and fry the shallots *or* spring onion gently until soft then stir in the flour and cook, stirring for 2 minutes. Bring stock and Madeira *or* wine to boil and blend into the shallots and flour. Add tomato purée and pepper. When simmering stir in the cream and continue simmering for several minutes until sauce is a light coating consistency. Check seasoning, add ham slices and reheat gently. Especially good served on a bed of cooked chopped spinach.

65

RIS DE VEAU GUIZOT

BRAISED SWEETBREADS

Preparation time 30 minutes plus 2 hours
soaking
Cooking time about 1 hour
To serve 3–4

You will need

1 lb. veal *or* lamb sweetbreads
2 slices pork fat for larding
2 oz. butter
1 medium-sized onion, sliced
2 large-sized carrots, sliced
1 stick celery, sliced
bouquet of thyme, bay and parsley, tied
salt and pepper
¼ pint (U.S. ⅝ cup) stock
¼ pint (U.S. ⅝ cup) dry white wine
2–3 tablespoons brandy
1 level teaspoon tomato purée
1 rounded teaspoon arrowroot

GARNISH

Pomme dauphine (optional) (see page 100)
6 small tomatoes, skinned
stuffed olives

Soak sweetbreads in cold water for 2 hours. Cover
with fresh cold water, bring to the boil, drain and
again cover with cold water. When cool carefully

Braised sweetbreads
Larding the blanched sweetbreads with bacon fat

remove as much of the skin and tissue as possible.
Thread a larding needle with ¼-inch strips of pork
fat and run several through each sweetbread,
leaving a little protruding. Melt butter in sauté
pan and stew the onion, carrots and celery gently
for 5 minutes. Lay prepared sweetbreads on top,
and add the herbs, seasoning, stock, wine, brandy
and tomato purée. Cover, and cook in a pre-
heated moderate oven (350°F. or Gas Mark 4),
for 40 minutes. Meanwhile cook tomatoes and
warm olives on lowest shelf of oven. Prepare and
cook the potatoes (if used). Drain sweetbreads and
arrange on hot dish. Strain cooking liquor into
small pan, boil to reduce to about ½ pint (U.S.
1¼ cups), add arrowroot slaked in a tablespoon of
cold water and bring to the boil. Check seasoning
and pour over sweetbreads. Garnish with the
potatoes (if used), tomatoes and olives.

ROGNONS SAUTÉ MADÈRE

SAUTÉ KIDNEYS WITH WINE

For 4 servings.
Heat 1 oz. butter and fry 3 calves or 8 lambs
kidneys, skinned and sliced for 3—4 minutes.
Remove and keep warm. Sprinkle 1 oz. flour into
pan, stir and cook for 1—2 minutes. Stir in ¼ pint
(U.S. ⅝ cup) stock, 3 tablespoons Madeira and
seasoning; simmer for 5 minutes. Replace the

Braised sweetbreads
Braising the sweetbreads on a bed of vegetables

kidneys and any juices. Add 1 teaspoon lemon juice and heat without boiling for several minutes. Serve sprinkled with chopped parsley.

Note
Use medium sherry in place of Madeira if wished.

CERVELLES AU BEURRE NOIR

BRAINS WITH BLACK BUTTER

Soak 2–3 sets calves brains in cold water to cover for at least 2 hours, changing the water several times. Put 1½ pints (U.S. 3¾ cups) water, 2 level teaspoons salt, 1 onion, bouquet of bay leaf, thyme and parsley, tied, and 2 tablespoons wine vinegar into a pan and simmer for 30 minutes; drain and cool. Carefully remove skin covering brains. Poach brains very gently in the cooled liquid for 20–25 minutes. Drain, cut in thick slices and keep warm. Heat 2 oz. butter in a small frying pan until nut brown, then pour over brains. Heat 2 tablespoons wine vinegar in the same pan and when sizzling pour over the brains and serve at once. Serves 4.

Note
Prepare lambs brains in the same way allowing 1 set per person but poaching for 15–20 minutes only.

COTES DE VEAU AUX HERBES

VEAL CHOPS WITH HERBS

Preparation time 10 minutes
Cooking time 25–30 minutes
To serve 4

You will need

4 veal chops, 1-inch thick
1 oz. butter
1 tablespoon oil
salt and pepper
2 tablespoons chopped shallots *or* spring onion
¼ pint (U.S. ⅝ cup) dry white wine
  or vermouth
1 rounded teaspoon chopped basil *or* tarragon,
  or ¼ teaspoon dried
scant ¼ pint (U.S. ⅝ cup) double cream

Dry chops. Heat butter and oil in frying pan and brown chops for 3–4 minutes each side. Season well and arrange in single layer in a flameproof casserole. Add shallots *or* spring onion to frying pan and cook *gently* for 5 minutes; add wine *or* vermouth and herbs and simmer 2–3 minutes. Add to chops, cover and cook in pre-heated oven (350°F. or Gas Mark 4), for 15–20 minutes. Dish chops. Add cream to casserole, stir and boil for several minutes; pour over chops.

Braised sweetbreads
Arranging the garnish

Braised sweetbreads
The finished dish

A delicately flavoured veal stew

BLANQUETTE DE VEAU

A DELICATELY FLAVOURED VEAL STEW

Preparation time 20 minutes
Cooking time 1¼ hours
To serve 4

You will need

1½ lb. shoulder *or* breast of veal
salt
half a lemon
1 carrot, quartered
1 onion, peeled
bouquet of bay leaf, thyme and parsley, tied
1 oz. butter
1 oz. flour
1 egg yolk
¼ pint (U.S. ⅝ cup) single cream
GARNISH
4 cooked mushrooms
few cooked peas
triangles of bread fried in butter

This is an excellent dish made from the cheaper cuts of veal.
Cut meat into 1-inch cubes. Put into a pan with 1 teaspoon salt, slice of lemon and cold water to cover. Bring slowly to the boil, drain and rinse (this is to blanch and whiten the meat). Return meat to rinsed pan with the prepared carrot, and onion, herbs and 1 pint (U.S. 2½ cups) water; cover and simmer for 1 hour or until tender. Strain off and reserve the liquid. Discard the vegetables and

herbs. Melt the butter in a saucepan, add flour and cook, stirring, for 1—2 minutes. Add ¾ pint (U.S. 1⅞ cups) of the liquid all at once, whisk until boiling, and boil for 3 minutes. Blend the egg yolk with cream, add *gradually* to the sauce, whisking briskly all the time. Add 1—2 teaspoons lemon juice, check seasoning and replace meat. Heat gently for 5 minutes but *do not boil*.
Serve garnished with mushrooms, peas and fried bread.

JARRET DE VEAU AU CITRON

STEWED KNUCKLE OF VEAL WITH LEMON

Preparation time 20 minutes
Cooking time 1¾ hours
To serve 4

You will need

2 lb. meaty knuckle of veal
little well seasoned flour
1 oz. butter *or* margarine
2 medium-sized onions, peeled and sliced
2 medium-sized carrots, sliced
¼ pint (U.S. ⅝ cup) dry white wine
1 lb. ripe tomatoes, skinned
1 level dessertspoon tomato purée
1 clove garlic, crushed
½ level teaspoon finely grated lemon rind
bouquet of thyme, bay and parsley, tied

Ask the butcher to saw the knuckle of veal in 2-inch pieces across the bone. Coat them with seasoned flour. Melt the butter or margarine in a saucepan and fry veal slowly till browned on all sides. Remove. Fry the prepared onion and carrot in same fat until golden, then replace the meat. Add the wine and bring to boil, then add tomatoes quartered and seeded, the tomato purée, garlic, lemon rind and herbs. Cover and simmer for 1½ hours. Remove the herbs and check seasoning. Dish the meat, and if necessary, reduce the sauce by rapid boiling before pouring over the meat.
Serve with buttered rice shaped in dariole moulds or cups.
A modern French recipe with an Italian flavour.

Stewed knuckle of veal with lemon

Liver with mustard and herbs

ESCALOPES DE VEAU A LA CRÈME

VEAL ESCALOPES WITH CREAM SAUCE

Preparation time 10 minutes
Cooking time 15 minutes
To serve 4

You will need

4 thin escalopes veal, about 3–4 oz. each
salt and pepper
little lemon juice
about 2 oz. butter
4 tablespoons dry white vermouth, white wine
  or Madeira (optional)
¼ pint (U.S. ⅝ cup) double cream
a few fresh tarragon leaves when available

Season the escalopes with salt, pepper and lemon juice. Heat 1½ oz. of the butter in a large frying pan and fry the escalopes two at a time, for 3—4 minutes on each side. Remove and keep hot. Add wine (if used) to the pan, stir and bubble briskly until reduced and syrupy. Add the cream and tarragon leaves, and stir gently until the sauce thickens very slightly. Replace the meat and heat gently for 1—2 minutes. Dish the escalopes and spoon the thickened sauce over.
This dish is often garnished with buttom mushrooms cooked à blanc (see page 98).

FOIE DE VEAU A LA MOUTARDE

LIVER WITH MUSTARD AND HERBS

Preparation time 10 minutes
Cooking time 5–6 minutes
To serve 4

You will need

4 slices calves *or* lambs liver, ½-inch thick
seasoned flour
2 tablespoons oil
2 level tablespoons French mustard
1 level tablespoon finely chopped shallot
  or spring onion
2 level tablespoons finely chopped parsley
fresh white breadcrumbs
2 oz. melted butter
GARNISH
orange slices
watercress

Fry liver slices, coated with flour, in hot oil for 1 minute on each side. Remove. Mix mustard, shallot *or* spring onion and parsley, adding drop by drop enough of the frying oil to make a 'creamy' mixture. Spread liver slices on each side with mustard mixture and coat with breadcrumbs, pressing on firmly. Lay slices in grill pan, spoon melted butter over and brown under a hot grill for 1—2 minutes; turn, baste with remaining butter and brown other side. Garnish with orange slices and watercress.

Lamb noisettes with artichoke hearts and peas
Boning the meat

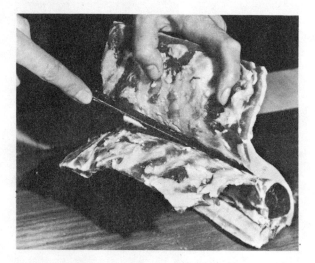

Lamb noisettes with artichoke hearts and peas
Rolling the boned meat

NOISETTES D'AGNEAU A LA CLAMART

LAMB NOISETTES WITH ARTICHOKE HEARTS AND PEAS

Preparation time 20 minutes
Cooking time 15 minutes
To serve 3

You will need

1 large best end of neck of lamb
salt and ground black pepper
2 teaspoons chopped fresh herbs, *or* ¼ teaspoon
   dried
2½ oz. butter
2 tablespoons Madeira wine
GARNISH
1 small can artichoke hearts
3 tablespoons cooked peas
miniature potato chips

The French way of making boneless 'nuts' of meat from the best end of neck raises this economical joint to the hostess level.

Ask the butcher to skin and chine the joint. Place on a chopping board, and using a sharp knife, cut the meat free first from the long rib bones then from the chine bone. Spread the boned meat flat, sprinkle with salt, ground black pepper and herbs. Roll up tightly from the thick end with flap wrapping once around the meat. Tie securely with fine string at 1½-inch intervals. Cut between the string to make 5 to 6 noisettes each 1 to 1½-inches thick.

Simmer the bones with vegetables, herbs and seasoning to make stock. All this can be done in advance.

To prepare the dish open the can of artichoke hearts and stand in boiling water to heat. Cook or reheat the peas and chips. Heat 1½ oz. butter in a heavy frying pan and fry the noisettes gently for 5—6 minutes on each side. Arrange round a hot serving dish, place a drained artichoke heart on each and fill with a few buttered peas. Arrange chips in centre of dish and keep warm while making sauce. Add ¼ pint (U.S. ⅝ cup) stock and the Madeira to the pan juices, stir well and boil for 2—3 minutes; season and stir in 1 oz. butter in small pieces.

Note

English butchers often prepare 'noisettes' from the loin of lamb (neck end).
If artichoke hearts are unavailable use mushroom caps sautéd in butter.

VARIATION

NOISETTES D'AGNEAU BERGERETTE
LAMB NOISETTES WITH ARTICHOKE HEARTS AND TOMATOES

Cook the noisettes of lamb as in the previous recipe. Serve them on croûtons of bread fried in butter and top them with fresh tarragon leaves.
Between the noisettes arrange hot canned artichoke hearts with a small whole grilled tomato in each. Serve with a Béarnaise sauce (see page 120).

ÉPAULE D'AGNEAU FARCI

STUFFED SHOULDER OF LAMB

Preparation time 20 minutes
Cooking time 2–2½ hours
To serve 8–10 portions

You will need

1 oz. butter
1 dessertspoon oil
2 oz. onion, finely chopped
4 oz. mushrooms, finely chopped
4 oz. boiled ham, chopped
1 level tablespoon chopped mixed fresh herbs
  or ½ teaspoon dried
salt and pepper
1 boned shoulder of lamb, about 3 lb.
little oil
1 large carrot, sliced
1 large onion, sliced
½ pint (U.S. 1¼ cups) meat stock

Prepare stuffing as follows. Heat butter and oil and fry onion gently until soft. Add mushrooms and stir and cook for a minute. Add ham, herbs and seasoning to taste and mix thoroughly. Lay meat flat, skin side down, and spread with stuffing. Roll meat into a cylindrical shape enclosing the stuffing completely. Tie round with string at 1½-inch intervals to hold in shape. Brush with oil. Place on a rack standing in a meat tin with the carrot and onion in the bottom. Roast in a pre-heated oven (350°F. or Gas Mark 4), allowing 30 minutes per lb. (including weight of stuffing) plus 30 minutes extra.

When cooked discard string and place meat on serving dish. Skim surplus fat from roasting tin, add stock and boil rapidly scraping up coagulated juices and mashing vegetables. Season, and strain into hot gravy boat.

CARRÉ D'AGNEAU PERSILLÉ

ROAST LAMB WITH PARSLEY

(Illustrated in colour on jacket)
Preparation time 20 minutes
Cooking time 1 hour
To serve 4

You will need

2 lb. best end *or* loin of lamb
salt and ground black pepper
1 clove garlic, sliced (optional)
3 oz. white breadcrumbs
1 heaped tablespoon chopped fresh parsley
2½ oz. melted butter

Pre-heat oven to (400°F. or Gas Mark 6). Rub meat with salt and pepper, and insert slices of garlic (if used) along underside of joint. Place on rack in tin and roast without any additional fat for 20 minutes. Mix crumbs, parsley and butter together and press thickly all over fat side surface of meat. Continue roasting for about 40 minutes until meat cooked and crumbs browned. Serve with gravy made in usual way. Tomatoes à la Provençale (see page 99) are good with this joint and can be cooked in the oven at the same time.

71

GIGOT D'AGNEAU BOULANGÈRE

LEG OF LAMB BAKERS STYLE

Preparation time 20 minutes
Cooking time 1¾ hours
To serve 6–8

You will need

3 lb. leg of lamb
salt and pepper
2 cloves garlic, peeled and sliced (optional)
1 oz. butter
1 tablespoon oil
8 oz. onions, sliced
2 lb. potatoes, thinly sliced
about ½ pint (U.S. 1¼ cups) stock
GARNISH
few chopped fresh herbs

Rub lamb with salt and pepper. Insert garlic pieces
(if used) around bone and under skin. Heat butter
and oil in a frying pan and fry the onions until
beginning to colour. Put meat in centre of ovenproof dish or roasting tin and arrange layers of
sliced onions and potatoes around it, seasoning each
layer lightly. Pour in stock to reach almost to top
of vegetables. Roast in centre of pre-heated moderate oven (350°F. or Gas Mark 4), for 1¾ hours.
Serve meat with potatoes around, or separately,
sprinkling the latter with chopped herbs.

ÉPIGRAMMES D'AGNEAU ST. GERMAIN

FRIED BREAST OF LAMB WITH PEAS

Preparation time 15 minutes
Cooking time about 2 hours
To serve 4

You will need

MEAT
2 lb. lean breast of lamb
1 level teaspoon salt
1 medium-sized onion, sliced
1 medium-sized carrot, sliced
1 stick celery, sliced
bouquet bay leaf, thyme and parsley, tied
COATING
seasoned flour
1 egg, beaten
dried white breadcrumbs
FRYING
oil or vegetable fat
GARNISH
purée of peas

This is the classic French method of cooking breast
of lamb. Put meat into a saucepan with the salt,
onion, carrot, celery and herb bouquet. Add water
just to cover. Cover and simmer gently until the
meat is tender, about 1½—2 hours. Drain meat and
remove all bones. Lay meat flat with a weighted
board on top, and leave until cold. Cut into 1-inch

Fried breast of lamb with peas
Cooked breast of lamb arranged around a purée of peas

...wide fingers, dip in seasoned flour and coat with egg and breadcrumbs. Fry in hot fat until golden on all sides, then drain on absorbent paper. Arrange around a mound of puréed peas and serve with lemon slices *or* a Béarnaise Sauce (see page 120).

PURÉE OF PEAS

Cook 1 lb. shelled mature peas in boiling salted water until tender. Drain and pass through a sieve or mouli-grater. Reheat purée with 1 oz. butter and seasoning.

Braised lambs tongues

LANGUES D'AGNEAU BRAISÉES AUX PETITS POIS

BRAISED LAMBS TONGUES

Preparation time 15 minutes
Cooking time 2 hours
To serve 4

You will need

4 lambs tongues
1 tablespoon oil
4 oz. slice fresh belly pork, diced
2 medium-sized onions, sliced
2 medium-sized carrots, sliced
4 tablespoons white wine
½ pint (U.S. 1¼ cups) stock
bouquet of thyme, bay leaf and parsley, tied
salt and pepper
1 oz. butter
1 can petits pois
GARNISH
1 tablespoon chopped fresh chervil *or* parsley

Scrub tongues and soak in cold water for at least 1 hour. Heat oil in a flameproof casserole and fry pork, onion and carrots until beginning to turn golden. Add wine and bubble briskly until reduced by half, then add stock, herbs and seasoning. Slice tongues lengthwise in half and place on top of vegetables. Cover closely and simmer very gently for 1¾ hours, or until tender. Add butter and drained peas; simmer another 20 minutes. Remove herb bouquet. Serve in the casserole sprinkled with fresh herbs *or* parsley.

FOIE SAUTÉ A LA BASQUE

LIVER IN BASQUE STYLE

Slice 1—2 aubergines ¼-inch thick; sprinkle with salt, leave to drain. Slice 3—4 onions, 12 oz. lambs liver; skin and slice 1 lb. tomatoes; crush 1 clove garlic. Heat 3—4 tablespoons oil and fry aubergines. Remove and keep warm. Add more oil, if necessary and fry onions, scatter over aubergines. Dip liver in seasoned flour and fry, place on top of onions. Add little more oil to the pan and fry tomatoes and garlic. Arrange in dish and sprinkle with parsley.

CHOUCROUTE GARNIE

SAUERKRAUT GARNISHED WITH BACON AND SAUSAGES

(Illustrated in colour opposite)
Preparation time 20 minutes
Cooking time about 4 hours
To serve 4–6

1½ lb. fresh sauerkraut*
4 oz. smoked streaky bacon
1½ oz. pork fat *or* butter
1 carrot, sliced
1 large onion, sliced
ground black pepper
4 crushed juniper berries (optional)
¼ pint (U.S. ⅝ cup) dry white wine ⎫
¾ pint (U.S. 1⅞ cup) stock *or* water ⎬ *or* all stock
1 lb. piece pickled belly pork ⎭
1 garlic sausage
4–6 frankfurters
plain boiled potatoes as required

* Sauerkraut is shredded white cabbage salted and fermented in wooden pickling tubs. It is available fresh from many delicatessen stores.

A robust country dish from Alsace. Put drained sauerkraut into a colander and steep in cold water for 20 minutes, changing the water 3 times. Drain and squeeze dry then unravel strands of cabbage as much as possible. Pre-heat oven to (300°F. or Gas Mark 2). Cut smoked bacon into strips 2-inches by ½-inch. Melt fat in a flameproof casserole and fry the bacon, carrot and onion lightly without browning. Stir in the sauerkraut and generous seasoning of black pepper. Add juniper berries (if used), wine and stock *or* water (*or* all stock). Bring to simmering point, cover tightly and transfer to centre of oven. Cook for 3 hours then bury the pork and garlic sausage in the sauerkraut and continue cooking another 1—1½ hours until meat is cooked and liquid absorbed. Add frankfurters 20 minutes before serving, and check seasoning. To serve spread the sauerkraut on a large hot dish. Arrange the thickly sliced pork and garlic sausage on top and surround with frankfurters and boiled potatoes. Serve alone, with French mustard and chilled lager beer or dry Alsation wine.

ROGNONS A LA BROCHETTE

LAMBS KIDNEYS ON A SKEWER

Preparation time 15 minutes
Cooking time 6–7 minutes
To serve 4

You will need

8 lambs kidneys
little oil
maître d'hôtel butter (see page 118)
GARNISH
watercress
small potato chips

Remove surrounding fat from kidneys. Place on a board with rounded side to your right hand. Nick skin in centre of curve and peel off towards core; draw out as much core as possible and cut off. Slice kidneys horizontally in half as far as the core, and lay flat. Impale kidneys 2 to a skewer and brush with oil. Grill fairly quickly, cut side first, for about 3 minutes each side. During cooking the kidneys will 'curl' forming hollows. Arrange skewers on a flat serving dish and put a small teaspoon of maître d'hôtel butter in the hollow of each kidney. Garnish with watercress and chips and serve at once.

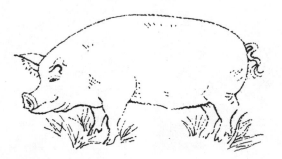

Choucroute garnie (Sauerkraut garnished with bacon and sausages)

Thon à la Provençale (Fresh tunny fish Provençal style)

To have no experience of the majestic tunny fish beyond the canned in oil variety is a sad omission in one's gastronomic life. The sight of gaily coloured tunny fishing boats chugging into harbour across a moonlit sea is one of the memorable sights and sounds of holidays on the Atlantic or Mediterranean coast of France. At the quayside you can watch the sardine bait still darting frantically to and fro in the brilliantly lit glass tanks while the rigid silver tunny are hauled ashore. Next day in the market thick steaks of pink fleshed tunny are sold for a song. In Brittany local folk sauté the fish in butter, adding after a while some sliced onion, chopped ripe tomato, bouquet of herbs and perhaps a little white wine. When the fish is tender, the wine reduced and the tomatoes pulped, it is scattered with chopped parsley and served with plain boiled potatoes. In Provence they add more than a touch of garlic, some lemon juice and ripe black olives, as in picture above and recipe on Page 79.

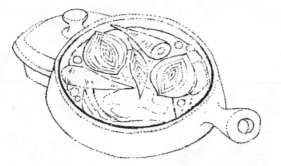

CASSEROLES

LES CASSEROLES

Long and very slow cooking in an earthenware casserole is the method used by generations of French women to create succulent dishes from cheaper cuts of meat and from poultry and game past its prime. The addition of wine, herbs and a clove or two of garlic, creates a savour which has made these simple dishes world famous. So much so that what were originally peasant dishes have in many cases become restaurant specialities. When you make them at home the wonderful fragrance that permeates the house has everyone clamouring 'how soon do we eat?'

Originally French casserole dishes were cooked beside a slow fire and some of the pots had a recessed lid to allow hot coals to be placed on top. Nowadays, even in France, the regional dishes have been largely replaced by modern enamelled cast iron ware. These are ideal because any initial frying can be done in the casserole before it is transferred to the oven. And many of them are elegant enough to send to the table. A tight fitting lid is essential to prevent undue evaporation and today's cooks use greaseproof paper or kitchen foil under the lid instead of the traditional flour and water paste seal. If French casseroles sometimes contain more and thinner gravy than others — this is because Frenchmen enjoy mopping up the surplus with hunks of bread!

Once prepared these slow cooking casseroles look after themselves, and with the help of an automatic time controlled oven are within the scope of working wives.

PERDRIX AUX CHOUX

CASSEROLED PARTRIDGE WITH CABBAGE

Preparation time 20 minutes
Cooking time   1–1½ hours
To serve   2

You will need

1 white winter cabbage about 1¾ lb.
2 oz. bacon fat *or* lard
1 small onion, finely chopped
1 stick celery, finely sliced
salt and ground black pepper
2 rashers unsmoked fat bacon
1 casserole partridge, oven ready
1 oz. butter

Wash and shred the cabbage. Melt the bacon fat *or* lard and fry the prepared onion and celery for a few minutes. Add the cabbage, stir frequently and continue frying until it begins to turn golden. Add seasoning and 2—3 tablespoons water, cover, and cook very gently for 30 minutes.

Meanwhile tie the rashers of bacon over the partridge. Melt the butter in a flameproof casserole and brown the partridge all over. When nicely browned surround and cover with the cabbage. Cover casserole closely and cook in a pre-heated slow oven (335°F. or Gas Mark 3), for 1—1½ hours. When tender serve partridge on a bed of the braised cabbage.

Note
Pheasant is very good cooked this way too.

Beef braised in wine
The raw ingredients

Beef braised in wine
The finished dish

BOEUF A LA MODE
BEEF BRAISED IN WINE

Preparation time 20 minutes
Cooking time about 4 hours
To serve 8–12

You will need

3–4 lb. piece of rolled silverside *or* topside
salt and ground black pepper
1 oz. lard
¾ pint (U.S. 1⅞ cups) robust red wine
1 or 2 split calves feet *or* knuckles of veal
4 oz. piece pork skin, diced
¾ pint (U.S. 1⅞ cups) stock *or* water
bouquet of bay leaf, thyme and parsley, tied
large clove garlic, peeled
2 tablespoons brandy (optional)
1 lb. carrots, sliced
1 lb. small onions, peeled
1 level tablespoon cornflour

Ask butcher to lard meat (i.e. run several thin strips of pork fat through length of joint). Rub meat all over with salt and pepper. Heat lard in oval flameproof casserole and brown meat on all sides. Drain off surplus fat. Add wine and bubble briskly for several minutes. Put calves feet *or* knuckles beside meat, and add the pork skin, stock *or* water, bouquet of herbs, garlic and brandy (if used). Cover with greaseproof paper and the lid. Cook in a pre-heated very slow oven (290°F. or Gas Mark 1), for 2½ hours. Turn meat over, add carrots and onions, and continue cooking another 1½ hours, or until meat very tender. Place meat on

serving dish with drained carrots and onions around; keep warm. Strain liquid into a saucepan, skim off fat, then boil rapidly until reduced to about 1 pint (U.S. 2½ cups). Blend cornflour with a little cold water, stir into gravy and simmer for several minutes. Check seasoning. Pour a little gravy over meat and vegetables and serve remainder in a sauce boat.

CÔTELETTES D'AGNEAU CHAMPVALLON
LAMB CHOPS WITH POTATOES AND ONIONS

Preparation time 15 minutes
Cooking time 1 hour
To serve 4

You will need

2 oz. butter *or* margarine
4 thick lamb chops
2 lb. potatoes, peeled
2 large onions, peeled
salt and pepper
2 cloves garlic, peeled (optional)
bouquet of parsley, thyme and bay leaf, tied
⅓ pint (U.S. ⅞ cup) meat cube stock

A savoury and practical family dish. Melt 1 oz. fat in a large frying pan and fry chops until lightly browned each side. Meanwhile slice potatoes and onions thinly, and pre-heat oven to (350°F. or Gas

78

Lamb chops with potatoes and onions

Mark 4). Remove chops and in the same fat fry half the potatoes and onions, turning frequently, until beginning to colour. Spread over bottom of wide casserole (or baking dish), and season with salt and pepper. Lay chops on top with garlic (if used) and herbs. Melt remaining butter in frying pan, fry rest of potatoes and onions and use to cover the chops. Season, and pour in the stock. Cover with lid or foil and cook in centre of oven for about 40 minutes or until tender. Remove herbs before serving.

THON A LA PROVENÇALE

FRESH TUNNY FISH PROVENÇAL STYLE

(Illustrated in colour on page 76)
Preparation time 15 minutes
Cooking time   about 30 minutes
To serve   4

You will need

2 tablespoons olive oil
6 button onions, peeled
1 lb. ripe tomatoes, peeled
1 bay leaf
1½ lb. fresh tunny fish
2 cloves garlic, peeled
salt and pepper
12 black olives
juice of ½ lemon
little chopped parsley

Pre-heat an oven to moderate (350°F. or Gas Mark 4). In a flameproof casserole heat the oil and fry the onions gently for a minute or so. Add the tomatoes cut in quarters, and bay leaf, and simmer gently for 10 minutes. Cut the tunny fish into 2-inch pieces and add to the tomato with the garlic cloves and salt and pepper to taste. Cover, transfer to centre of oven and cook for about 20—25 minutes. A few minutes before end of cooking stir in the olives, and lemon juice. Serve very hot, sprinkled with parsley, with crusty French bread to mop up the sauce.

LA DAUBE BÉARNAISE

BEEF STEWED BEARN STYLE

Preparation time 15 minutes plus time to marinate
Cooking time   about 4 hours
To serve   4–6

You will need

2 lb. lean topside *or* leg of beef
½ pint (U.S. 1¼ cups) full bodied red wine
2 tablespoons olive oil
salt and ground black pepper
bay leaf and sprig thyme, tied
large clove garlic
4 oz. piece fresh pork rind
little flour
1 large onion, sliced
2 large carrots, sliced
6 oz. unsmoked streaky bacon, diced
¼–½ pint (U.S. ⅝–1¼ cups) stock

Cut meat into pieces about 2½-inches square by 1-inch thick. Put into china basin with wine, oil, seasonings, herbs and garlic. Stir, cover and leave in cool place to marinate overnight. When ready to cook put pork rind in bottom of casserole. Strain meat, roll each piece in flour and put on top of pork rind. Add onion, carrots, diced bacon, marinade complete with herbs, a little more seasoning and enough stock almost to cover the meat. Seal casserole tightly with foil and lid. Cook in a pre-heated very slow oven (290°F. or Gas Mark 1), for about 4 hours. Skim off surface fat, check seasoning and serve in casserole, with purée potatoes. Reheats excellently.

LES PETITS SALÉ
AUX LENTILLES

BOILED BACON WITH LENTILS

Preparation time 20 minutes
Cooking time 2 hours
To serve 5–6

You will need

1½ lb. joint collar bacon
1 oz. dripping *or* bacon fat
about 12 button onions, peeled
ground black pepper
1 lb. large brown lentils
1 stick celery, halved
2 carrots, cut lengthwise
bouquet of fresh herbs, tied
2 cloves garlic, crushed
GARNISH
sprigs of parsley

Cover bacon joint with cold water, bring slowly
to boil, then drain, rinse and pat dry. Melt fat in
a deep flameproof casserole. Put in the joint, the
onions and a seasoning of black pepper (no salt).
When onions begin to brown, add the lentils,
celery, carrots, herbs and garlic. Cover with cold
water, and simmer very slowly, tightly covered,
for about 2 hours. When the lentils are cooked
take out the bacon, remove the carrots, celery and

Boiled bacon with lentils

herbs and strain the lentils. Arrange the lentils
around a hot serving dish, with more separately
cooked onions if liked, and arrange thickly sliced
bacon in the centre. Garnish with sprigs of parsley.

POULET EN COCOTTE
BONNE FEMME

CHICKEN WITH
POTATOES AND BACON

Preparation time 15 minutes
Cooking time 1¼–1½ hours
To serve 4–6

You will need

1 oven ready chicken, 2½–3 lb.
salt and pepper
1 tablespoon oil
2 oz. butter
8 button onions, peeled
6 oz. slice unsmoked bacon, cut in strips
4 oz. button mushrooms (optional)
1 lb. potatoes, cut into small cubes
1 tablespoon chopped chives *or* parsley

A delicious way of cooking chicken. Dry the chicken
and season generously inside. Heat the oil and butter

Chicken with potatoes and bacon

in a flameproof cocotte large enough to contain bird and vegetables. Put in the chicken and over moderate heat brown bird on all sides — this will take about 15 minutes. After first 5 minutes add the onions and bacon. Now add mushrooms (if used) and the potatoes; turn gently mixing them with the buttery juices, onions and bacon. Cover pan tightly, transfer to a pre-heated moderate oven (350°F. or Gas Mark 4), and cook for 1—1¼ hours or until tender. Serve from the casserole sprinkling potatoes with chopped chives *or* parsley.

NAVARIN OF LAMB

LAMB STEW WITH VEGETABLES

Preparation time 20 minutes
Cooking time about 2 hours
To serve 4

You will need

1½ lb. shoulder of lamb, without bone
2 tablespoons olive oil
1 level teaspoon sugar
1 level tablespoon seasoned flour
¾ pint (U.S. 1⅞ cups) stock *or* water
1 level tablespoon tomato purée
1 clove garlic, crushed
bouquet of bay leaf, thyme and parsley, tied
4 small onions, peeled
3 small carrots, quartered
3 medium-sized potatoes, peeled and
    quartered
4–5 oz. cooked *or* canned peas

A Navarin is especially good when made with young spring vegetables.
Cut meat into 1½-inch cubes. Heat oil in flameproof casserole and fry meat until lightly browned. Drain off excess fat. Sprinkle sugar into the casserole and stir over moderate heat until lightly caramelised. Add flour and stir until pale brown, then stir in the stock *or* water, tomato purée, garlic and herbs. Bring to the boil. Cover and cook in a pre-heated slow oven (310°F. or Gas Mark 2), for 1 hour. Check seasoning and add vegetables, pushing them beneath sauce. Cover and cook for another hour or until tender. Add peas for last 5 minutes. With the Navarin serve hot French bread, and a rosé or light red wine.

LE CASSOULET

The name Cassoulet derives from Cassol d'Issel, originally a clay cooking pot from the town of Issel, near Castelnandary. The recipe has many variations, but always contains several of the following ingredients — smoked bacon, pork, garlicy sausages, pieces of preserved goose, pork rind, mutton, pig's feet — all simmered in a capacious earthenware pot with haricot beans and herbs.

CASSOULET TOULOUSAIN

BEAN POT TOULOUSE STYLE

Preparation time 15 minutes plus overnight
    soaking of beans
Cooking time 4–5 hours
To serve 7–8

You will need

1½ lb. dried haricot beans
1 large onion, sliced
3 cloves garlic, crushed
1 lb. gammon, a cheap cut
bouquet of thyme, bay leaf and parsley, tied
1 lb. fresh belly pork
1 breast of mutton *or* lamb
2–3 pieces preserved goose (optional)
1 lb. garlic sausage
salt and pepper if necessary

Soak beans overnight in water to cover. Next day drain and put into a large casserole with the onion, garlic, gammon and herbs. Cover with fresh water, put on lid and cook in a pre-heated slow oven (310°F. or Gas Mark 2), for 3—4 hours, until beans are almost cooked. Meanwhile in the same oven, in an open roasting tin, cook the pork, breast of lamb and goose (if used). Drain beans and reserve liquor. Cut all meats into small pieces, discarding skin and bones. Cut sausage into thick slices. In a deep earthenware pot arrange alternative layers of beans and meat, starting and finishing with beans. Pour in enough bean liquor to reach half way up. Cook, uncovered, in a slow oven for another hour or until liquid has been absorbed. Check seasoning. Serve with green salad and finish meal with cheese *or* fresh fruit. Excellent cold weather dish for hungry young folk.

BOEUF EN DAUBE A LA MARSEILLES

BEEF WINE STEW MARSEILLE STYLE

Preparation time 20 minutes
Cooking time about 4 hours
To serve 5–6

You will need

2 lb. lean chuck *or* blade steak
½ pint (U.S. 1¼ cups) robust red wine
2 tablespoons olive oil
ground black pepper
bouquet of thyme, bay leaf and parsley, tied
1–2 cloves garlic, crushed
4 oz. onions, sliced
4 oz. carrots, sliced
6 oz. unsmoked streaky bacon
12 oz. tomatoes, peeled and seeded
2 oz. mushrooms, sliced (optional)
8 black olives, stoned

Cut the chuck *or* blade steak into pieces about 2-inches square and 1-inch thick. Put into a china bowl with the wine, oil, black pepper, herbs, garlic, onions and carrots. Stir well, cover, and leave in a cool place to marinate for 4 hours or overnight. Next day cut the streaky bacon into strips and cover the bottom of a 2-pint casserole with half

Beef wine stew Marseille style

of it. Put the meat on top with the vegetables and wine from the marinade.

Add the peeled and seeded tomatoes and cover with remaining bacon. Cover tightly and cook in centre of a pre-heated very slow oven (290°F. or Gas Mark 1), for 4 hours or longer. Add the prepared mushrooms (if used) and well washed and stoned olives for last 30 minutes. Skim off fat if necessary and check seasoning. Serve in the casserole, with purée potatoes.

JARRET DE BOEUF EN DAUBE

LEG OF BEEF STEWED WITH WINE

Preparation time 20 minutes
Cooking time 3¼ hours
To serve 4

You will need

1½ lb. top leg of beef, without bone
1 tablespoon olive oil
2 thick slices green bacon, diced
1 large onion, sliced
1 large clove garlic, crushed
bouquet parsley, thyme, and bay leaf, tied
¼ pint (U.S. ⅝ cup) robust red wine
¼ pint (U.S. ⅝ cup) stock *or* water
salt and ground black pepper

Cut the beef into 2-inch cubes. Heat the oil and prepared bacon in a flameproof casserole and when bacon fat begins to run add the onion and cook gently for several minutes. Arrange meat on top, add garlic, bouquet of herbs, wine, stock *or* water and seasoning to taste. Bring to boil, cover closely with foil and lid and cook in a pre-heated very slow oven (290°F. or Gas Mark 1), for at least 3 hours.
Serve with creamed potatoes, and crusty bread to mop up the gravy.
This, like all daubes, improves with reheating.

Stuffed cabbage
Inserting the sausage meat and liver mixture between
each cabbage leaf

Stuffed cabbage
The finished dish

CHOU FARCI

STUFFED CABBAGE

Preparation time 20 minutes
Cooking time 3 hours
To serve 4

You will need

2 lb. cabbage with firm heart
salt
12 oz. pork sausage meat
4 oz. chicken *or* lambs liver, finely chopped
1 large onion, sliced
2 large carrots, sliced
1 bay leaf
4 tablespoons white wine
½ pint (U.S. 1¼ cups) stock
3 rashers smoked streaky bacon

Discard loose outer leaves and wash cabbage.
Blanch in boiling salted water for 5 minutes. Drain
upside down in a colander. When cool enough to
handle cut out hard stalk and open out the leaves.
Mix sausage meat and liver together and insert
a little between each cabbage leaf. Reform cabbage
and tie with tape. Put the onion, carrots, bay leaf,
wine and stock into a deep casserole and place the
cabbage, stalk end down, on top. Lay bacon rashers
over cabbage and cover pan closely. Cook in a pre-
heated slow oven (290°F. or Gas Mark 1), for
3 hours or longer, basting now and then. Serve
the cabbage surrounded with carrots.

FAISAN A LA VALLEY D'AUGE

PHEASANT WITH
APPLES AND CREAM

Preparation time 15 minutes
Cooking time 1 hour
To serve 3

You will need

1 oz. butter
1 tablespoon oil
1 young pheasant, oven-ready
3 oz. onion, finely chopped
3 tablespoons Calvados *or* brandy
¼ pint (U.S. ⅝ cup) game *or* chicken stock
8 oz. dessert apples, peeled and cored
¼ pint (U.S. ⅝ cup) double cream
salt and pepper
GARNISH
apple rings fried in butter

Heat butter and oil in a flameproof casserole and
brown pheasant slowly all over. Cook onion at the
same time. Drain off surplus fat. Pour Calvados
or brandy into heated ladle, set alight and pour
over pheasant. When flames die add stock, sliced
apples, cream and seasoning. Cover tightly and
simmer very gently for about 40–50 minutes.
Carve and arrange pheasant on serving dish. Strain
sauce and boil rapidly until reduced to coating
consistency. Check seasoning, pour over pheasant.
Garnish with fried apple rings.

COQ AU VIN ROUGE

CHICKEN IN RED WINE

(Illustrated in colour opposite)
Preparation time 20 minutes
Cooking time   1½ hours
To serve   4

You will need

3 lb. chicken, jointed or quartered
1 small onion, sliced
salt and ground black pepper
4 oz. slice unsmoked streaky bacon
1½ oz. butter
1 tablespoon olive oil
12 button onions, peeled
1 clove garlic, crushed
bouquet of bay leaf, thyme and parsley, tied
2 tablespoons brandy
½ bottle red wine, preferably Burgundy
4 oz. button mushrooms
THICKENING
1 oz. flour
1 oz. softened butter
GARNISH
crescents of bread fried crisp in butter

This famous dish well repays the extra attention needed while cooking. Remove back bone and leg shanks from chicken and simmer them for 30 minutes with the giblets, onion, seasoning, and water just to cover. Strain and reserve stock. Cut bacon into ¼-inch strips and dry chicken pieces. Heat butter and oil in a wide sauté pan, and fry chicken joints, bacon and onions, turning as necessary, until golden, about 12 minutes. Add the garlic, herbs and seasoning, cover, and cook over *low* heat for 10 minutes. Drain off surplus fat. Pour brandy into heated ladle, ignite and pour over chicken. Shake pan gently until flames die down. Add wine and stock and when boiling cover pan

tightly and simmer very gently over low heat or transfer to a pre-heated oven (350°F. or Gas Mark 4), for 1 hour. Remove chicken and keep warm. Discard herbs. Boil liquid rapidly until reduced to about ½ pint (U.S. 1¼ cups). Cream flour and butter to a paste (this is beurre manie used for thickening liquids) and add to the pan in walnut size pieces, whisking briskly all the time until sauce is medium thick. Check seasoning, add mushrooms and replace chicken. Heat gently for 10 minutes. Serve from casserole or arrange in a shallow dish and garnish with the crescents of fried bread. Serve with plain boiled potatoes tossed in butter and chopped parsley. Drink a similar wine to that used in the cooking.

Note

Coq au Vin can also be made with white wine. When a special wine is used the dish takes the name of the wine, for example Coq au Chambertin, Coq au Reisling or Coq au Vin Jaune.

LE PORC MARENGO

PORK STEWED WITH WINE AND TOMATOES

Cut 1¼ lb. of boneless shoulder, or fillet of pork into 1-inch cubes. Fry golden in a little lard in a flameproof casserole; remove. In same fat fry 2 sliced onions and when golden work in 1 tablespoon flour and cook 1 minute. Stir in ⅓ pint (U.S. ⅞ cup) white wine, half a bay leaf, an 8 oz. can peeled tomatoes and seasonings of salt, sugar and ground black pepper. When boiling, replace meat, cover closely, and cook in a slow oven (300°F. or Gas Mark 1) for 1½ hours. Serve with boiled rice.

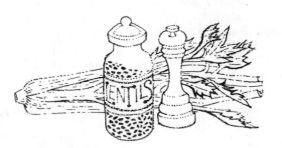

Coq au vin rouge (Chicken in red wine)

Poulet rôti au beurre Provençal (Chicken with olives and peppers)

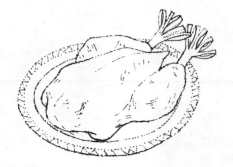

POULTRY AND GAME

LES VOLAILLES ET LE GIBIER

The wonderful succulence and flavour of French poultry dishes is legendary. A plump tender bird is considered an ideal companion for a bottle of fine vintage wine and on these occasions the bird is roasted in butter — quite plainly but perfectly. Roasting on a turning spit is preferred, otherwise by the oven method given below. In the South a roast chicken will be surrounded with colourful vegetables or garlic flavoured stuffed tomatoes. Cooking in butter in a covered casserole is another excellent way of adding extra succulence to poultry and game, and a large oval cast iron enamelled pan similar to that shown on page 11 is indispensible for cooking 'en cocotte'. The French choose the method of cooking to suit the age of the bird, grilling or sautéing for the very young, roasting or casseroling for the mature but tender, and simmering with vegetables and herbs for a good fat hen.

When jointing a chicken the chefs method is to cut the bird into 8 pieces, but for home cooking appearance and flavour are better if the bird is cut into quarters. You will find more recipes for poultry and game in the chapter on Casseroles.

POULET RÔTI AU BEURRE
CHICKEN ROASTED IN BUTTER

Preparation time 10 minutes
Cooking time about 1¼ hours
To serve 4–5

You will need

3 lb. roasting chicken, oven ready
salt, pepper
sprigs fresh *or* dried herbs
2 oz. softened butter
1 small onion, sliced
1 small carrot, sliced
GARNISH
watercress
miniature chip potatoes

Dry chicken. Sprinkle inside with salt; insert herbs and 1 oz. butter. Spread rest of butter over skin and place chicken on its side in roasting tin. Cook in centre of pre-heated oven (375°F. or Gas Mark 5), for 20 minutes, turn on to other side, baste, cook another 20 minutes, then turn breast up, baste and cook until tender. This should take 1—1¼ hours, by which time the skin should be deep golden and crisp. Meanwhile simmer giblets with onion, carrot, seasoning and water just to cover. Dish chicken. Strain giblet stock into roasting pan, stir to loosen residue and boil rapidly till reduced to ½ pint (U.S. 1¼ cups). Garnish with watercress and chips and hand gravy separately. Serve a rosé or light red wine.

VARIATION
POULET RÔTI AU BEURRE PROVENÇAL
CHICKEN WITH OLIVES AND PEPPERS
(Illustrated in colour opposite)

Grill sweet red peppers gently for 15—20 minutes turning until pepper is soft and skin blackened. Rinse off black skin, halve peppers and remove seeds. Arrange around chicken; garnish with black olives and stuffed green olives.

To crush a clove of garlic

Casserole chicken Corsica style

POULET COCOTTE CORSOISE

CASSEROLE CHICKEN CORSICA STYLE

Preparation time 15 minutes
Cooking time 1¼–1½ hours
To serve 4–5

You will need

3 lb. plump chicken, oven ready
salt and pepper
1 oz. butter *or* margarine
4 oz. slice belly pork, diced
6 oz. green olives
4 tomatoes, peeled and quartered
2 oz. mushrooms, sliced
1 clove garlic, crushed
1½ lb. new *or* waxy potatoes, diced
fat for frying

Dry the chicken and season the inside with salt and pepper. Heat 1 oz. fat in an oval flameproof casserole, add the diced pork, and brown the chicken on all sides. This will take about 15 minutes.
Cover the olives with cold water, boil for 2 minutes, then drain. Put the olives, the prepared tomatoes and mushrooms around the chicken, add garlic and seasoning to taste. Cover tightly and simmer very gently for about 1—1¼ hours. Meanwhile fry the diced potatoes slowly, in shallow pan, in 2 or more instalments, until golden and cooked.
Serve chicken with the olives, tomatoes, mush-

rooms and fried potatoes around, and juices poured over.

POULET NORMANDE

CHICKEN NORMANDY STYLE

Preparation time 20 minutes
Cooking time 1 hour
To serve 4

You will need

2–2½ lb. frying chicken
2 level tablespoons seasoned flour
2½ oz. butter
4 oz. unsmoked streaky bacon, diced
1 small onion, chopped
2 sticks celery, cut up
½ lb. apples, roughly chopped
¼ pint (U.S. ⅝ cup) cider
½ pint (U.S. 1¼ cups) chicken stock
3—4 tablespoons double cream
seasoning of salt, pepper and sugar to taste
GARNISH
triangles of bread fried in butter

Cut chicken into serving pieces and dust with some of seasoned flour. Melt butter in a large saucepan and fry bacon and chicken pieces until chicken lightly browned both sides; remove. Fry onion, celery and apple until beginning to soften. Sprinkle in remaining flour, stir and cook for several minutes. Stir in cider and stock and bring

Chicken Normandy style

Devilled grilled chicken

to the boil. Return chicken pieces to pan, cover closely and simmer gently for 45 minutes. Dish chicken and keep hot. Press sauce through a strainer, return to pan and, if necessary, boil until reduced to a coating consistency. Stir in cream, adjust the seasoning, and pour over chicken. Garnish with triangles of bread fried crisp and golden in butter.

POULET GRILLÉ A LA DIABLE

DEVILLED GRILLED CHICKEN

Preparation time 10 minutes
Cooking time 25—30 minutes
To serve 2

You will need

2 oz. butter
2 tablespoons oil
2 plump chicken halves, 12 oz. each
salt
2 rounded tablespoons French mustard
1 oz. finely chopped shallot *or* spring onion
⅛ teaspoon dried thyme
pinch cayenne
fresh white breadcrumbs for coating
GARNISH
watercress

Melt butter with oil in a small pan. Dry chicken, brush liberally with fat and arrange skin side down

in a grill pan without rack. Place pan 6-inches beneath pre-heated grill and cook chicken for about 10 minutes each side, brushing with fat and sprinkling lightly with salt twice during cooking. Meanwhile beat together mustard, shallot *or* spring onion, thyme and cayenne in a basin, adding drop by drop 2 tablespoons of the melted fat. Spread chicken joints all over with this mixture, then roll in breadcrumbs, pressing crumbs on firmly. Replace joints skin side uppermost in grill pan, sprinkle with remaining melted fat and grill for 5—6 minutes, until crisp and golden. Serve, garnished with watercress.

COQUELETS SUR CANAPÉS

BABY CHICKEN ON LIVER CANAPES

Allow one small chicken (or pigeon, quail or partridge) per person. Truss, wrap in fat bacon and roast in the usual way. Prepare a ¼-inch thick rectangle of bread to fit under bird and fry until golden in melted butter. Chop the livers *very* finely with a little fresh pork fat then blend in a flavouring of brandy *or* Madeira, and if available a little foie gras. Spread on one side of bread and grill for 1 minute. Dish each bird on a canapé and surround with sautéed button mushrooms, and sprigs watercress. Spoon a little Madeira flavoured gravy over each bird just before serving.

89

FAISAN A LA CRÈME

PHEASANT IN CREAM SAUCE

Preparation time 5 minutes
Cooking time 1 hour
To serve 4

You will need

1 young pheasant, drawn and trussed
salt and pepper
1½ oz. unsalted butter
1 medium-sized onion, quartered
¼ pint (U.S. ⅝ cup) double cream
a few drops lemon juice
GARNISH
canned *or* frozen petit pois

Season the pheasant with salt and pepper. Heat the butter in a heavy saucepan or flameproof casserole and put in the pheasant breast down with the onion around. Cover closely and cook over *low* heat, turning now and then to cook on all sides, for about 30 minutes. Acidulate the cream by stirring in a few drops of lemon juice then pour over the pheasant. Continue cooking very gently for another 20—30 minutes, or until tender. Arrange the pheasant on a bed of hot drained peas. Whisk the sauce briskly until smooth, check the seasoning and pour over the pheasant.

Pheasant in cream sauce

Duckling with orange

CANETON A L'ORANGE

DUCKLING WITH ORANGE

Preparation time 20 minutes
Cooking time about 2 hours
To serve 4—5

You will need

4—5 lb. duckling
salt and ground black pepper
1 small onion
3 oranges
1 oz. butter
1 rounded tablespoon granulated sugar
⅓ pint (U.S. ⅞ cup) chicken stock
juice half lemon
2 tablespoons Cointreau *or* brandy

Sprinkle duck inside and out with salt and pepper. Insert onion and 3 thinly pared strips orange rind into body cavity. Place duckling breast up on rack in roasting tin, with washed giblets in tin under rack. Smear breast with butter and roast in a pre-heated moderate oven (350°F. or Gas Mark 4), allowing 20—25 minutes per lb. of weight. Meanwhile remove orange rinds thinly from 1 orange, cut into matchstick strips, cover with water and boil for 5 minutes; drain. Cut skinless segments from one orange and squeeze juice from rest. In a small saucepan heat sugar with 2 table-spoons of water until caramelised, add chicken stock and heat gently until caramel dissolved. When cooked dish duck and keep warm. Skim excess fat from roasting tin, add chicken stock, orange and lemon juice, and liqueur; stir and boil until well reduced. Check seasoning and strain over duck.

Sprinkle with orange strips and garnish with segments.

Duck with olives

DINDE FARCIE AUX MARRONS

TURKEY STUFFED WITH CHESTNUTS

Preparation time 20 minutes
Cooking time about 3 hours
To serve 10–12

You will need

12 oz. chestnuts
7–8 lb. turkey, oven ready
salt and pepper
12 oz. cocktail sausages *or* sausage meat balls
1 onion, sliced
1 carrot, sliced
4 oz. slice belly pork, diced
bouquet thyme, bay leaf and parsley, tied
2 oz. softened butter
GARNISH
watercress

Make small slit in shell of each chestnut and bake in hot oven for 10 minutes or until shells split. While still hot remove shell and inner skin. Season inside of turkey liberally with salt and pepper and insert chestnuts mixed with sausages *or* sausage meat balls. Place turkey in a roasting tin standing on a bed consisting of the giblets, sliced onion and carrot, diced pork, herbs and 5 tablespoons water. Spread the skin of the turkey with softened butter and cover loosely with double greaseproof paper or foil. Cook in a pre-heated very moderate oven (350°F. or Gas Mark 4), for about 3 hours, removing the greaseproof or foil for the last 30 minutes. When cooked dish bird. Add ½ pint (U.S. 1¼ cups) water to giblets in roasting tin (and a little wine if handy) and simmer for 10 minutes. Strain into gravy boat.

Garnish the turkey with watercress.

CANETON AUX OLIVES

DUCK WITH OLIVES

Preparation time 15 minutes
Cooking time 1½–2 hours
To serve 4–5

You will need

1 young duckling, about 3 lb. oven ready
1½ oz. butter *or* margarine
1 level tablespoon flour
¼ pint (U.S. ⅝ cup) dry white wine
¼ pint (U.S. ⅝ cup) chicken stock
bouquet of thyme, bay leaf and parsley, tied
ground black pepper
6 oz. green olives

Dry the duck thoroughly and season lightly inside. Melt fat in a flameproof oval casserole, put in the duck and cook over moderate heat until well browned on all sides. This will take 15—20 minutes. Remove duck and pour off all but 1½ tablespoons of fat. Stir in flour and cook and stir for 1—2 minutes. Stir in wine and stock and when boiling replace duck. Add herbs and a little pepper (no salt because of olives). Cover tightly and cook in a pre-heated moderate oven (350°F. or Gas Mark 4), for 1¼—1½ hours. Meanwhile remove stones from olives, cover with cold water and boil for 2 minutes; drain. Add olives to duck and cook another 15 minutes or until tender. Discard herbs and check seasoning. Serve duck with olives around and sauce poured over.

LAPIN À LA CHASSEUR

RABBIT HUNTER STYLE

Preparation time 15 minutes plus soaking time
Cooking time 1½ hours
To serve 4

You will need

1 young rabbit, 2–3 lb., jointed
1 tablespoon oil
1 oz. butter
1 onion, chopped
1½ level tablespoons cornflour
¼ pint (U.S. ⅝ cup) dry white wine
½ pint (U.S. 1¼ cups) chicken stock
1 level tablespoon tomato purée
bouquet thyme, parsley and bay leaf, tied
salt and pepper to taste
4 oz. mushrooms, sliced
little chopped parsley, to garnish

Soak rabbit joints in cold salted water for several hours. Drain, dry well. Heat oil and butter in wide flameproof casserole, fry rabbit and onion over medium heat, turning frequently, until lightly browned. Sprinkle in cornflour, stir and cook for 1 minute. Stir in wine and bubble for a few seconds, add stock, tomato purée, herbs and seasoning. Bring to boil, cover tightly, simmer for 1—1¼ hours. Add mushrooms for last 15 minutes. Discard herb bouquet, check seasoning. Serve rabbit from

Rabbit hunter style

casserole, sprinkled with parsley.

POULET SAUTÉ AU VIN BLANC

CHICKEN IN CREAM AND WINE SAUCE

Preparation time 5 minutes
Cooking time 30–40 minutes
To serve 4

You will need

2½ lb. frying chicken, quartered
1 oz. butter
1 tablespoon oil
salt and white pepper
1 oz. finely chopped shallot *or* onion
¼ pint (U.S. ⅝ cup) dry white wine
½ pint (U.S. 1¼ cups) double cream

Dry chicken joints. Heat butter and oil in wide pan with lid, and sauté chicken briskly. Season, cover pan and cook over *low* heat, 25—30 minutes. Remove chicken and keep warm. Add shallots *or* onion to pan and cook 1 minute. Add wine and boil rapidly, stirring occasionally until reduced to half. Stir in cream, replace chicken, and simmer until sauce thickens slightly. Serve with buttered rice.

Note

This elegant but simple dish is a speciality of various regions in France famous for white wine. Although you can use any dry white wine the recipe has a particular distinction when made with a specific wine as suggested below. Whatever wine you use, a similar wine should be drunk with the dish, and the recipe takes its name from the wine used.

POULET SAUTÉ AU CHAMPAGNE

Use a dry, non vintage, champagne as they do in Rheims, Epernay and other centres of the champagne producing area.
Garnish the dish with button mushrooms cooked á blanc, see page 98.

POULET SAUTÉ AU REISLING

Use a flavoursome reisling wine as they do in Ribeauvillé, Riquewihe and other wine centres of Alsace.

POULE A L'IVOIRE

BOILED FOWL
WITH CREAM SAUCE

Preparation time 20 minutes
Cooking time 2–3 hours
To serve 6–8

You will need

4 lb. plump boiling fowl, oven ready
1 lemon
2 carrots, scraped
3 leeks *or* 2 onions, peeled
1 stick celery, cut up
salt and pepper to taste
1 teaspoon lemon juice
6 oz. button mushrooms
1 oz. butter *or* margarine
1 oz. flour
¾ pint (U.S. 1⅞ cup) stock from chicken
2 egg yolks
2–3 tablespoons double cream

Rub skin of bird with cut lemon. Put into a large pan with prepared carrots, leeks *or* onions, celery, salt and pepper. Add hot water just to cover. Cover tightly and barely simmer until tender, about 2—3 hours. Simmer mushroom caps for 5 minutes in a little salted water and the lemon juice. When tender drain chicken, remove skin and carve into joints. Arrange joints on dish and keep warm. Make sauce as follows. Melt fat, add flour and cook stirring for 2 minutes. Add stock, whisk until boiling and simmer 10 minutes. Remove from heat. Blend egg yolks and cream together, and *whisk* into the sauce *little* by *little*. Reheat gently, but *do not boil*. Coat chicken with sauce and garnish with drained mushrooms.

VARIATION
POULE AU POT HENRI IV
KING HENRY'S CHICKEN IN THE POT

This is the dish that Henry of Navarre wished all his subjects could enjoy every Sunday. Stuff the neck end of a plump boiling fowl with sausage meat and simmer as in the recipe above with the addition of a small quartered cabbage, some fresh herbs and peppercorns. One hour before chicken is cooked add two ½-inch thick slices pickled belly pork and if wished extra vegetables. Serve the fowl reposing on a large platter with pork on either side and firmer vegetables grouped around. The remaining

Boiled fowl with cream sauce

vegetables finely chopped are reheated in the chicken stock for soup next day.

POULET RÔTI A L'ESTRAGON

CHICKEN WITH TARRAGON
CREAM SAUCE

Preparation time 10 minutes
Cooking time about 1½ hours
To serve 4–6

You will need

3–4 lb. plump chicken, oven ready
salt and ground black pepper
3 oz. butter
1 heaped tablespoon chopped *fresh* tarragon
4 tablespoons double cream

Dry chicken thoroughly. Sprinkle inside with salt and pepper and insert 1 oz. butter creamed with half tarragon. Spread chicken with remaining butter and roast, first on one side and then on the other, in a pre-heated moderately hot oven (375°F. or Gas Mark 5), for 1 hour. Turn breast up, spoon cream over bird and continue roasting another 20—30 minutes, basting with pan juices. Carve chicken and arrange on serving dish. Add remaining tarragon (or more to taste) to pan juices, season, and whisk briefly to blend cream and buttery juices. Pour over chicken and serve.

PERDRIX A LA VIGNERONNE

PARTRIDGES WITH GRAPES

(Illustrated in colour opposite)
Preparation time 30 minutes
Cooking time   about 25 minutes
To serve   2–4

You will need

8 oz. small white grapes
2 young partridges, oven ready*
salt and pepper
2 oz. butter
1–2 teaspoons lemon juice
GARNISH
fresh bay leaves (optional)

* Young quails *or* pigeons may be cooked the
same way.

Skin and pip half the grapes. Season the birds
inside with salt and pepper and insert ½ oz. butter
and 4—5 grapes in each. Melt the remaining butter
in a flameproof casserole and brown the birds on
each side. Leave the birds breast down, cover the
casserole and cook in the centre of a pre-heated
oven (400°F. or Gas Mark 6), for about 20 minutes
or until tender. Dish the birds and keep warm.
Press the unpeeled grapes through a sieve and stir
the resulting liquid into the buttery juices in the
casserole. Add the lemon juice and remaining
peeled grapes, and heat gently without boiling.
Check the seasoning. Spoon grapes around birds
and pour the sauce over.
Garnish with fresh bay leaves, if available.

POULET A LA BASQUAISE

CHICKEN BASQUE STYLE

Preparation time 20 minutes
Cooking time   45 minutes
To serve   4

You will need

2½ lb. roasting chicken *or* 4 chicken quarters
salt
1½ oz. butter
1 tablespoon oil
4 ripe tomatoes
1 large green pepper
4 oz. mushrooms, chopped
¼ pint (U.S. ⅝ cup) white wine
2 oz. ham *or* bacon, diced
GARNISH
chopped fresh parsley

Cut chicken into serving portions and sprinkle
with salt. Heat the butter and oil in a heavy pan
and fry the chicken pieces over gentle heat, until
golden both sides, about 10 minutes. Meanwhile
skin and seed the tomatoes and chop the flesh.
Discard seeds from green pepper and cut the flesh
into fine strips. Add tomatoes, pepper, mushrooms,
wine and ham *or* bacon to the chicken, cover
closely and simmer gently for 30—40 minutes.
Remove chicken to serving dish and kept hot.
If necessary reduce sauce to a coating consistency
by boiling rapidly without the lid for a few minutes.
Season and pour over the chicken. Sprinkle with
chopped parsley and serve with plain boiled rice.

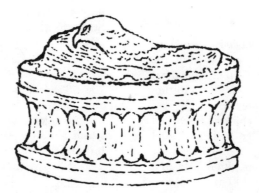

Perdrix à la vigneronne (Partridge with grapes)

Partridge stuffed with grapes is one of those ex-quisitely simple dishes one falls upon by chance in some country auberge where food is treated with loving care. You will probably be in a wine pro-ducing area, for surely it needs no flight of fancy to believe that such a dish was created by a vine grower's wife to do justice to her husband's prowess as marksman and vigneron. Or you may prefer to argue that it was a case of divine coincidence that the grapes were ripening at the same time as the young birds were at their best.

In any case you'll find the recipe on the opposite page, and in case you find partridge an elusive bird, I have seen the same recipe using quails de-monstrated by a master chef at the Paris Cordon Bleu School of Cookery.

It can be used for pigeon too provided they are truly young and tender.

Le gratin Dauphinois (Potatoes baked with cream)

Dauphine is famous for its gratin dishes. There you will find bubbling golden gratins of crayfish tails, of mushrooms, chard, and pumpkin to mention just a few.

But of them all none is more famous and more subject to controversy than the simple gratin of potatoes known as le gratin Dauphinois. Happily all the authorities on the great regional dishes of France give recipes for it and are agreed on the basic ingredient of thinly sliced potatoes arranged in layers in a thickly buttered garlic rubbed shallow dish and that the gratin should be dotted with butter before being baked in a slow oven until the potatoes are soft and creamy.

VEGETABLES

LES LÉGUMES

The French choose and cook vegetables with immense care. In the country, time and space are lavished on the vegetable rather than the flower garden and in towns housewives shop daily for the freshest market produce. Vegetables are seldom, if ever plain boiled. They are cooked in various ways always with the object of preserving and enhancing their natural flavour. More often than not a choice young vegetable dressed with a sauce, or with melted butter sharpened with lemon juice, is served on its own. Sometimes hot, sometimes cold such a dish is frequently the first course. A stuffed vegetable is another favourite first course, and aubergine, peppers, tomatoes, cabbage, mushrooms and artichoke hearts are all favourite subjects for filling with a minced meat or savoury rice mixture.

It is true the French do not worry overmuch about preserving vitamins when cooking vegetables and will tell you frankly they consider colour and flavour are more important. For this reason they plunge green vegetables into vast quantities of fast boiling salted water until *just* cooked. If vegetables are to be served cold, or have to be kept waiting, further cooking is stopped by plunging into ice cold water for a few moments — a process known as 'refreshing'. When required the vegetables are reheated gently in butter.

Overcooking and keeping hot are the quickest ways to ruin vegetables, say the French, and how right they are.

LE GRATIN DAUPHINOIS
POTATOES BAKED WITH CREAM

(Illustrated in colour opposite)
Preparation time 15 minutes
Cooking time about 1½ hours
To serve 4

You will need

1¼ lb. waxy potatoes, peeled
1½ oz. butter
small clove garlic, crushed (optional)
salt, pepper and grated nutmeg
2 oz. Gruyère cheese, grated
½ pint (U.S. 1¼ cups) single cream

A golden potato dish to serve with grills and casseroles.
Slice the potatoes ⅛-inch thick or less (the mandoline will do this rapidly) and soak in cold water. When required drain and *dry* the potatoes on a cloth. Mix the butter and garlic (if used) and use a third to grease a *shallow* ovenproof dish. Spread half the potatoes over the bottom, and sprinkle with the seasonings and half the cheese. Dot with half the remaining butter. Arrange remaining potato slices evenly on top, sprinkle with seasonings and cheese, and pour the cream over. Dot with remaining butter. Cook in a pre-heated slow oven (310°F. or Gas Mark 2), for about 1½ hours, until potatoes are creamy and surface golden.

VARIATION
GRATIN SAVOYARD
POTATOES BAKED WITH STOCK

A less rich dish in which beef stock is used instead of cream. This gratin may be cooked in a hotter oven for less time, if wished.

RATATOUILLE NICOISE

AUBERGINES, ONIONS, TOMATOES AND PEPPERS STEWED IN OIL

Preparation time 20 minutes
Cooking time 1 hour
To serve 3–4

You will need

2 large aubergines, wiped
6 tablespoons olive oil
2 large onions, sliced
2 red *or* green sweet peppers, halved
2 cloves garlic, crushed
12 oz. tomatoes, peeled and chopped
½ level teaspoon dried basil
salt and ground black pepper

Cut unpeeled aubergines into ½-inch dice, put into colander, sprinkle with salt. Cover, leave to drain for 1 hour. Heat oil in a sauté pan; fry onions until soft. Discard seeds from peppers, cut flesh into strips. Add peppers, drained aubergines and garlic to onions, cover, and stew very gently for 30 minutes. Add tomatoes, basil and seasoning; continue cooking gently, without lid, for 15—20 minutes, until vegetables are soft and surplus moisture evaporated. Serve hot as a separate dish, or cold as an hors-d'oeuvre.

CHOU ROUGE AUX MARRONS

RED CABBAGE WITH CHESTNUTS

Cut 1¼ lb. red cabbage into thin shreds. Heat 3 oz. pork *or* bacon dripping in a flameproof casserole; fry 3 oz. peeled and sliced onion until golden. Add prepared cabbage and 6 oz. peeled and sliced cooking apples, mix well. Add ¾ pint (U.S. 1⅞ cups) meat stock, seasoning and bring to the boil. Cover, transfer to a pre-heated slow oven (310°F. or Gas Mark 2) and cook for 1 hour. Meanwhile slit skin of about 20 chestnuts and roast in oven until shell and skin can be peeled off. Cut into quarters and add to cabbage mixture. Continue cooking for another 1—1½ hours, until vegetables are soft and liquid has evaporated. Serve hot in the casserole.

CHAMPIGNONS A BLANC

STEWED MUSHROOMS

Preparation time 5 minutes
Cooking time 5 minutes
To serve 2–4

You will need

4 oz. fresh mushrooms, washed
4 tablespoons water
⅛ teaspoon salt
½ tablespoon lemon juice
½ oz. butter

Leave mushrooms unpeeled, either slice, quarter or leave whole. In a small saucepan bring water, salt, lemon juice and butter to the boil. Add mushrooms. Cover, cook over moderate heat for 5 minutes, tossing pan now and then. Use for sauces and garnishes.

HARICOTS VERTS A LA PROVENCALE

FRENCH BEANS WITH TOMATO

Preparation time 10 minutes
Cooking time 15–25 minutes
To serve 3–4

You will need

1 lb. haricots verts, fresh *or* frozen
2 tablespoons olive oil
2 oz. onion, coarsely chopped
1 clove garlic, crushed
3 ripe tomatoes, skinned and quartered
salt and ground black pepper

Top and tail beans, rinse in cold water. Cook in boiling salted water until just tender, about 10—15 minutes. (Prepare frozen beans according to label directions). Heat oil in pan, fry onion gently for 5 minutes. Add garlic, tomatoes and salt and pepper; cover, and simmer until cooked to a purée. Add well drained beans, mix lightly; heat *gently* for 5—10 minutes. Garnish with chopped parsley. A good dish to serve on its own.

CHAMPIGNONS A LA CREME

MUSHROOMS WITH CREAM

Preparation time 5 minutes
Cooking time   10 minutes
To serve   3

You will need

8 oz. button mushrooms
1 oz. butter
1 dessertspoon oil
salt
1 rounded teaspoon flour
¼ pint (U.S. ⅝ cup) double cream
squeeze lemon juice
1 teaspoon chopped parsley

Wash, but not peel, the mushrooms and remove the stalks.
Over low heat melt the butter and oil in a shallow flameproof dish, put in the mushrooms, stalk side uppermost, and sauté gently for 5 minutes. Sprinkle with salt. Draw mushrooms to side of pan, and stir flour into buttery juices. Stir all together over low heat for 1—2 minutes then pour in cream and allow to bubble briskly until cream thickens, another 1—2 minutes. Finally stir in a squeeze of lemon juice.
Sprinkle with parsley and serve immediately on their own, after the main course or as a meal starter. May also be served on toast.

TOMATES A LA PROVENCALE

TOMATOES WITH BREADCRUMBS AND GARLIC

(Illustrated in colour on the jacket)
Preparation time 5 minutes
Cooking time   15 minutes
To serve   4

You will need

4 large firm ripe tomatoes
salt and pepper
1 large clove garlic, crushed
1 oz. chopped parsley
1 oz. dry white breadcrumbs
3–4 tablespoons olive oil

Cut the tomatoes horizontally in half and make a shallow depression in the centre. Sprinkle with salt and pepper.
Mix together the crushed garlic, parsley and breadcrumbs and add sufficient oil to moisten well. Fill the tomatoes with this mixture and arrange side by side in a shallow fireproof dish. Bake for 15 minutes in a pre-heated moderately hot oven (400°F. or Gas Mark 6).
Alternatively grill gently until the tomatoes are tender then increase the heat to brown the surface. These are excellent served with roast or grilled chicken, lamb or grilled meats.

Scooping out potato for fried potato balls

POMME PARISIENNE

FRIED POTATO BALLS

Preparation time 15 minutes
Cooking time 15 minutes
To serve 3

You will need

4 large potatoes, peeled
2 oz. butter
1 tablespoon oil
salt

With a small ball cutter (illustrated above) cut out as many balls as possible from each potato and drop into cold water. Use trimmings for other recipes. Cook balls in boiling salted water for 5 minutes, drain; dry thoroughly. Heat butter and oil in a frying pan, and fry potatoes over moderate heat, rolling them around the pan from time to time, until evenly golden brown, about 10 minutes. Drain and sprinkle with salt.

CHOU-FLEUR
AU BEURRE NOIR
CAULIFLOWER WITH 'BLACK' BUTTER

Break 1 medium-sized cauliflower into flowerets and cook in boiling salted water until just tender, about 10–15 minutes. Drain well and arrange in a hot gratin dish with the flower heads uppermost. Heat 2 oz. butter in a small frying pan until nut brown; immediately pour over cauliflower. Swill out pan with 1 tablespoon wine vinegar and pour this too over cauliflower. Scatter 1 sieved hard-boiled egg yolk on top and serve hot.

POMME DAUPHINE

POTATO PUFFS

Preparation time 25 minutes
Cooking time 10 minutes
To serve 4

You will need

1 lb. floury potatoes, peeled
1 recipe Choux pastry (see page 148)
½ oz. butter
salt, pepper and grated nutmeg
deep fat for frying

Cook potatoes in boiling salted water until tender. Make Choux pastry. Drain potatoes, shake in pan over heat until very dry and fluffy. Sieve, and beat in butter, seasoning and the Choux pastry. Mix well. All this can be done in advance. When ready to cook heat fat to frying temperature (a cube of stale bread should frizzle gently when dropped into fat). Drop Dauphine mixture in teaspoonfuls into hot fat, fry until puffed and golden. Remove, drain on absorbent paper.

NAVETS GLACÉS

GLAZED TURNIPS

Peel 1 lb. very small even-sized turnips (if large cut into halves or quarters). Cook in boiling lightly salted water until *just* tender, then drain off all but 2–3 tablespoons water. Add 1 oz. butter and 2 level teaspoons castor sugar and heat gently, shaking the pan frequently until a slightly sticky brown glaze is formed. Spoon the glaze over the turnips and use to garnish a dish of roast or grilled lamb or duck.

CHOUX VERTS AU GRATIN

CABBAGE AU GRATIN

Preparation time about 15 minutes
Cooking time about 30 minutes
To serve 4

You will need

1¼ lb. white winter cabbage, trimmed and
  washed
½ pint (U.S. 1¼ cups) Béchamel sauce
  (see page 120)
salt, pepper, grated nutmeg and dry mustard
1 oz. Gruyère cheese, grated
1 oz. dry white breadcrumbs
1 oz. butter, melted

Quarter the cabbage and cook in boiling salted
water until *just* tender. Drain, press as dry as
possible; chop *very* finely. Meanwhile make a thin-
nish Béchamel sauce and season well with salt,
pepper, nutmeg and mustard. Add cabbage and
heat to boiling point. Off heat stir in cheese; turn
into a 2-inch deep heatproof dish. Sprinkle with
breadcrumbs and melted butter. Brown in a very
hot oven or under grill.

Note
Brussels sprouts may be cooked in the same way.

Cabbage au gratin

ASPERGES AU NATUREL

BOILED ASPARAGUS — HOT OR COLD

Preparation time 20 minutes
Cooking time 15–20 minutes
To serve 4

You will need

2 lb. plump fresh asparagus spears
one of the sauces indicated below

Asparagus is usually served as a course on its own,
as a meal starter or after the main course. The
French method of cooking asparagus is economical
as the maximum amount of stalk is made edible.
Wash spears and with a sharp knife *peel* rather
than scrape away tough white skin, working from
root towards tip. Trim stalks to equal lengths and
tie in 4 bundles. Choose a pan wide enough to hold
the bundles *horizontally* and half fill with salted
water. When boiling lower the asparagus in gently,
and *simmer*, uncovered, for 15—20 minutes. Remove
each bundle, drain on a folded clean teacloth and
cut the string.

TO SERVE HOT

Separately hand either Hollandaise sauce (see page
121) *or* Sauce Maltaise or Mousseline (see below)
or Beurre au Citron (see page 118).

TO SERVE COLD

Serve with one of the following sauces. Sauce
Vinaigrette (see page 109), Sauce Ravigote (see
page 109) *or* Mayonnaise (see page 119). Always
lay finger bowls when serving asparagus.

SAUCE MOUSSELINE

Follow recipe for Hollandaise sauce (see page 121),
just before serving fold in 4 tablespoons of lightly
whisked double cream.

SAUCE MALTAISE

Follow recipe for Hollandaise sauce (see page 121),
add 1 tablespoon orange juice and 1 teaspoon
finely grated rind to the finished sauce.

POIVRONS FARCIS AU RIZ

PEPPERS STUFFED WITH RICE

Preparation time 15 minutes
Cooking time   about 1 hour
To serve   4

You will need

2 oz. butter *or* margarine
3 oz. long grain rice
½ pint (U.S. 1¼ cups) water
salt and pepper
half bay leaf
sprig thyme
4 sweet peppers
2 large tomatoes, peeled and chopped
1 tablespoon oil
2 medium-sized onions, sliced
2 cloves garlic, chopped

Melt 1 oz. fat in a saucepan, add rice and stir for
a minute. Add water, salt and pepper, bay leaf
and thyme. Cover closely and simmer for 10 minutes only. Meanwhile cut a slice off stem end of
the peppers, and carefully discard all the seeds.
Three quarters fill each pepper with rice and
replace the lids. Cut tomatoes in half and squeeze
out some of the juice. Heat the remaining fat and
the oil in a flameproof casserole, add the stuffed
peppers and the onions and cook over moderate
heat, moving around gently, for 10 minutes, then

add the tomatoes, garlic and a little salt. Cover
and cook over low heat for 15 minutes. Carefully
turn the peppers and continue cooking, uncovered,
another 15—30 minutes until completely cooked
and surplus moisture evaporated. Serve hot or cold.

PETITS POIS AU LARD

PEAS WITH BACON

Preparation time 15 minutes
Cooking time   40–45 minutes
To serve   4–6

You will need

2 thick slices pickled belly pork (4 oz.)
3 oz. button onions, peeled
1 level tablespoon flour
½ pint (U.S. 1¼ cups) water
1 lb. mature shelled peas, frozen or fresh
pepper and salt to taste

Cut pork into ¼-inch strips. Heat in a saucepan
until fat begins to run, adding ½ oz. butter if
necessary. Add onions and toss and cook in the
fat until golden. Sprinkle in flour, cook until this
too is golden, then add the water and stir until
boiling. Add peas, pepper, and salt if necessary.
Cover and simmer gently for about 30 minutes.
Serve without draining.

Peppers stuffed with rice

Peas with bacon

CARROTTES A LA CHANTILLY
CREAMED CARROTS WITH PEAS

Preparation time 5 minutes
Cooking time 15–20 minutes
To serve 4

You will need

1 lb. carrots, scraped
5 oz. carton frozen peas
2 oz. butter
4 tablespoons double cream
pepper and salt

Cook the carrots in boiling salted water until just tender, slicing them thinly *before* cooking if large but *after* cooking if new. Cook the peas according to directions on packet. Melt 1 oz. of the butter in a saucepan and toss the well drained carrots in it until butter absorbed, then add the cream and pepper and salt to taste. Cover, and keep warm. Drain the peas and toss with remaining 1 oz. butter. Arrange the carrots around the outside of a shallow serving dish and pile the peas in the centre.

Note

Instead of carrots you could use diced turnips, celeriac, Jerusalem artichokes *or* pieces of tender celery. Drain well before tossing in butter.

FENOUIL GRATINÉ
FENNEL WITH CHEESE

Preparation time 5 minutes
Cooking time 40 minutes
To serve 4

You will need

4 small bulbs of Florentine fennel
1½ oz. butter *or* margarine
salt and pepper
2 oz. Gruyère cheese, grated

Fennel root has a delicate aniseed flavour which combines with cheese to make an original first course. Cut the fennel bulbs in half lengthwise and drop into a large pan of boiling salted water. Simmer until tender, about 30 minutes. Drain. Arrange in a well greased gratin dish and sprinkle lightly with salt and pepper, and thickly with cheese. Dot with remaining fat and brown lightly in a hot oven or under the grill. Serve hot.

Note

Gratiné is a favourite way of serving any cooked vegetables tossed in butter *or* coated with sauce, then sprinkle evenly with breadcrumbs *or* grated cheese and dotted with butter. Grill until surface is golden brown and crusty.

Creamed carrots with peas

Fennel with cheese

POIREAUX A LA NIÇOISE

LEEKS STEWED
WITH OIL AND TOMATOES

Preparation time 10 minutes
Cooking time 25–30 minutes
To serve 2–4

You will need

4 plump white leeks
3 tablespoons olive oil
salt and pepper
2 large ripe tomatoes, skinned
1 clove garlic, crushed
1 tablespoon chopped parsley

Wash and trim the leeks. Heat the oil in a sauté pan and lay leeks side by side in the oil. Season with salt and pepper. Cover pan tightly and cook over *very low* heat until tender, about 15–20 minutes, turning once or twice. Remove leeks and arrange in shallow dish. Chop tomatoes and add to the oil remaining in the pan, with the garlic and parsley. Simmer two minutes then pour over the leeks. Serve cold as an hors-d'oeuvre, or hot with roast or grilled meat.

AUBERGINE AUX TOMATES

AUBERGINE WITH TOMATOES

Preparation time 1 hour
Cooking time 30–40 minutes
To serve 4

You will need

2 plump fresh aubergine
12 oz. ripe tomatoes, peeled
olive oil
small clove garlic
salt and ground black pepper
tomato purée
dry white breadcrumbs

Wipe aubergine and cut into ½-inch thick rounds. Spread in a colander, sprinkle with salt and leave to drain for 1 hour. Chop tomatoes and cook gently in 1 tablespoon of oil, with garlic, and seasoning to taste, for 10–15 minutes, until reduced to a thick purée.

Dry aubergine slices and fry gently in shallow oil until golden each side, about 5 minutes.

Add more oil during cooking as the aubergine absorb it. Arrange slices, in single layer in a gratin dish. Spread a spoonful of tomato purée over each slice, sprinkle with breadcrumbs and moisten with a trickle of oil. Cook, uncovered, in a pre-heated moderate oven (350°F. or Gas Mark 4), for 30–40 minutes.

These succulent slices are equally good hot or cold, served alone as a first course, or with the meat.

COURGETTES A LA NIÇOISE

BABY MARROWS
WITH TOMATOES

Wash, dry and top and tail 1 lb. courgettes (baby marrows). Slice them ¼-inch thick, sprinkle with salt and leave in a colander to drain for 1 hour. Dry in a cloth.

Heat 2 tablespoons olive oil in a heavy pan, add the dried courgettes and 1 crushed clove of garlic. Cover and cook *gently* until soft, turning now and then, for about 15 minutes.

Add 8 oz. ripe tomatoes, peeled and roughly chopped. Cook over a low heat until the tomatoes are soft and pulped.

Sprinkle with freshly milled pepper and 1 tablespoon chopped fresh parsley *or* tarragon and turn into a serving dish.

Serve hot or cold, alone, or with lamb, veal or chicken.

Poireaux à la Niçoise (Leeks stewed with oil and tomatoes

HERBS FOR FRENCH COOKING

Herbs are indispensible if you want to capture the real flavour and fragrance of French cooking. Anyone who possibly can should grow, in addition to rows of parsley, at least the seven varieties on these pages. The full fragrance comes mainly from the volatile oils released when *fresh* herb leaves are chopped, pounded or fried in oil. Oil incidentally is a wonderful 'carrier' of flavours. Other herbs much used in French cooking, particularly in the South, are marjoram, rosemary and basil.

Dried herbs are invaluable but only when fresh are unobtainable. They should be bought in small quantities and kept tightly stoppered in a cool, preferably dark, place. When in France, try to obtain some bunches of dried Provençal herbs as they are more aromatic than English herbs.

Two classic mixtures of herbs used time and time again in French recipes are:

BOUQUET GARNI

Consisting of 2—3 stalks of parsley, a sprig of thyme and a bay leaf, all tied together with a thread to facilitate removal before the dish is served. Optional additions are a small stick of celery, sprig of marjoram and, in Provençal cookery, a piece of dried orange peel.

FINES HERBES

Consisting of equal quantities of chopped fresh parsley, chives, chervil, and when available, tarragon.

Chervil — Cerfeuil

Tarragon — Estragon

CHERVIL (CERFEUIL)

Grown from seed sown in rotation in spring or summer, or indoors in winter. A dainty herb of the parsley family much used for soups, sauces and omelettes.

TARRAGON (ESTRAGON)

A perennial grown in sun from rooted cuttings planted in spring in light, well drained soil. Much used for chicken, aspic jelly, tomatoes, salads, fish and sauces. Make tarragon vinegar by leaving a large sprig permanently in a bottle of good wine vinegar. True French variety is best.

CHIVES (CIBOULETTE)

Grown from a clump of bulbs planted in autumn or spring. Increased by division, and successful in window boxes. Used fresh to impart subtle onion flavour to salads, soups, omelets and sauces.

FENNEL (FENOUIL)

Common fennel is a perennial grown readily from seed sown in a sunny position in spring. The feathery foliage is used for garnishing, or chopped

Fennel — Fenouil

in sauces and salads. Dried stalks used for burning under grilled fish. The bulbous root used as a vegetable comes from the Florentine variety which is more difficult to cultivate.

BAY LEAVES (LAURIER)

Grown from a small plant, planted in spring in a sheltered position. Needs protection in cold weather. Small specimens may be grown in tubs. Use fresh or dried leaves in sauces, stews and marinades. Indispensible in a 'bouquet garni'.

THYME (THYM)

A perennial grown from rooted cuttings planted in spring in light sandy soil. A pungent aromatic herb much used fresh or dried to flavour stews, stuffings and meat and poultry dishes generally. Indispensible for a 'bouquet garni'.

SORREL (OSEILLE)

A perennial grown from seed sown in early spring preferably in moist humid rich soil. The fleshy leaves impart an astringent flavour to soups and omelettes; also served as a purée. The true French variety has best flavour.

Sorrel — Oseille

SALADS

LES SALADES

Salads are considered an important item of diet in France. An absolutely plain green salad, the 'salade verte', appears every day at either the mid-day or evening meal. It is served on a separate plate either at the same time, or immediately after, the meat or main course. Lettuce is the normal 'salade verte' but others such as watercress and chicory (known in France as endive) are used frequently, while young dandelion leaves (pissenlits), lambs lettuce (mache) and curly endive (known as chicorées) are popular for winter salads. Salad vegetables are always carefully washed and dried, then tossed with an oil and vinegar, or oil and lemon juice dressing at the last possible moment before serving. The dressing should taste of oil with only a hint of acidity; this is particularly important when a fine wine is drunk with the meal. Individuality is achieved by using flavoured vinegars and fresh herbs. The addition of garlic to dressings and salads is a matter of personal preference; it is general practise in the South of France but not in the North.

A subtle 'touch' of garlic is added by rubbing the bowl with a cut clove or adding a crushed clove to the dressing. Simple salads consisting of a single dressed vegetable such as potato, tomato, cucumber, carrot or red cabbage are usually served as part of a mixed hors-d'oeuvre.

More elaborate 'salades composées' using a mixture of ingredients and sometimes including meat, shell fish or poultry, are usually served alone as an hors-d'oeuvre (Salade Niçoise and Salade de Moules, see pages 110, 112), or sometimes after the meat course. Exactly where in the meal the salad is served is not nearly as important as attractive arrangement and careful dressing.

SALADES VERTES

GREEN SALADS

Preparation time 10 minutes
To serve 3–4

You will need

1 lettuce *or* other salad greens
Vinaigrette dressing (see page 109)

A French green salad consists of plain lettuce or other salad greens dressed with an oil and vinegar dressing. It is served on a separate plate with or after the meat or main course. Although so simple it needs careful preparation. Wash the lettuce *or* salad greens in cold water then shake in a salad basket or clean teacloth until quite dry. If possible put into a polythene bag and crisp in the refrigerator. Mix the Vinaigrette dressing in the salad bowl. Add the lettuce *or* salad greens, which if large may be torn but never shredded, and immediately before serving toss very lightly but thoroughly with the dressing until each leaf is glistening with oil.

VARIATIONS

LAITUE MIMOSA

GREEN SALAD WITH HARD-BOILED EGG

Prepare salad as above and serve sprinkled with the sieved yolk of a hard-boiled egg.

SALADE AU CHAPON

GREEN SALAD WITH GARLIC

For garlic lovers. Well rub a thick slice of bread

on *both* sides with a cut clove of garlic, then sprinkle it with oil. Place in bottom of salad bowl with the lettuce on top. Just before serving add the dressing and toss lightly.

COEUR DE LAITUE

LETTUCE HEARTS

Cut tender lettuce hearts into quarters and dress with Vinaigrette or with melted butter flavoured with garlic and lemon juice.

SALADE À L'ANGEVINE

DANDELION SALAD

Tear crisp lettuce leaves into pieces and mix with a few dandelion leaves and some diced Gruyère cheese. Immediately before serving, dress with Vinaigrette with herbs (see opposite).

SAUCE RAVIGOTE

VINAIGRETTE WITH HERBS

Add 1 teaspoon each finely chopped shallot, capers, gherkins and 2 tablespoons chopped fresh herbs.

VINAIGRETTE À L'OEUFS

VINAIGRETTE WITH EGGS

Prepare vinaigrette with garlic and lemon juice. Then stir in the yolk of a soft-boiled egg and finally the chopped white of egg.

SAUCE GIBICHE

VINAIGRETTE WITH EGG AND GHERKIN

Stir herb vinaigrette into a sieved hard boiled egg yolk. Add chopped egg white and gherkin.

SAUCE VINAIGRETTE

OIL AND VINEGAR DRESSING

Preparation time 5 minutes
To serve 4

You will need

¼ level teaspoon salt
large shake pepper
1 tablespoon wine *or* herb flavoured vinegar
 or lemon juice
3–5 tablespoons olive *or* vegetable oil
OPTIONAL ADDITIONS
⅛ teaspoon dry mustard
small clove crushed garlic
1 tablespoon chopped fresh herbs (parsley,
 tarragon, chives, chervil)

This is the dressing invariably used for green salads. Mix salt, pepper and mustard or garlic (if used) and vinegar *or* lemon juice in the bottom of a salad bowl until salt has dissolved. Add the oil, beating briskly. Just before using stir in the herbs. *Alternatively* put all ingredients into a screw top jar and shake vigorously for half a minute. Useful for mixing larger quantities as surplus can be stored in the jar in a refrigerator for several weeks.

VARIATIONS

VINAIGRETTE À LA CRÈME

LEMON AND CREAM DRESSING

Mix with lemon juice instead of vinegar and replace oil with thin cream.

SALADE DE BOEUF PARISIENNE

BEEF AND POTATO SALAD

Preparation time 15 minutes plus 30 minutes
 for marinading
To serve 4

You will need

12 oz. — 1 lb. sliced boiled beef
Vinaigrette with herbs (see above)
1 lb. potato salad (see page 112)
2 hard-boiled eggs, quartered
2–3 firm tomatoes, quartered
cress *or* watercress
a few thin onion rings (optional)

A recipe for using up the cold beef from a pot-au-feu, or any sliced cold meat.
Marinade the meat in the Vinaigrette with herbs for 30 minutes.
When ready to serve arrange the sliced boiled beef on a flat platter with the potato salad on either side.
Decorate the edges of the dish with the eggs, tomatoes and cress. Scatter a few onion rings over the meat if wished, and sprinkle with any remaining Vinaigrette.

SALADE DE MOULES

MUSSEL SALAD

Preparation time 20 minutes
To serve 4

You will need

2 pints (U.S. 7½ cups) fresh mussels
Vinaigrette with herbs (see page 109)
1 lb. cooked waxy potatoes, diced
5–6 oz. cooked peas
1 stick tender celery, sliced
1 large tomato, cut in six

Prepare and open the mussels as for Moules Marinière (see page 56). Reserve six mussels in shells for garnishing then discard the rest of the shells. Put the Vinaigrette in a salad bowl, add potatoes, peas, mussels and celery and toss lightly together. Just before serving garnish with reserved mussels and tomato slices.

VARIATION

MOULES À LA FECAMPOISE

Prepare celeriac with mustard flavoured mayonnaise (see page 119). Arrange in shallow dish; top with freshly cooked cold mussels. Sprinkle with parsley.

SALADE AUX NOIX

NUT AND CHEESE SALAD

Preparation time 10 minutes
To serve 4

You will need

Vinaigrette dressing (see page 109)
1 lettuce, washed and crisped
1 head chicory
2 oz. chopped walnuts
4 oz. Gruyère cheese, diced

Make the Vinaigrette in the salad bowl. Add the torn lettuce leaves, chicory cut in 1-inch wide pieces, nuts and cheese. Just before serving toss lightly with the dressing.

SALADE AU LARD

BACON SALAD

Wash and dry 12 oz. young dandelion leaves *or* curly endive; put in shallow bowl. Cut 4 oz. smoked streaky bacon into ¼-inch strips, fry until fat begins to run. Pour *hot* bacon *and* fat over greens. Add 2—3 tablespoons wine vinegar to frying pan, swill around; when *boiling* pour over salad. Toss lightly together. Add salt, if necessary and serve at once.

Mussel salad

Potato, celery and ham salad

SALADE CAUCHOISE

POTATO, CELERY AND HAM SALAD

Preparation time 25 minutes
To serve 3–4

You will need

1 lb. new *or* waxy potatoes
1 head celery
2 tablespoons milk
$\frac{1}{4}$ pint (U.S. $\frac{5}{8}$ cup) double cream
salt and white pepper
1 tablespoon lemon juice
1 thick slice cooked ham
a little chopped parsley
1 tablespoon chopped truffle (optional)

Boil potatoes in their jackets in salted water until
just tender. Drain, and when cool, peel and cut
into matchstick sized strips. Using the tender stalks
only cut the celery into similar sized strips and add
to the potato. Add the milk to the cream, whip
until thick, season well with salt and pepper and
stir in the lemon juice. Add to the potato and
celery and mix delicately but thoroughly. Arrange
in a salad bowl. Cut the ham into thin strips and
sprinkle over the salad, with the parsley. Chill
until ready to serve. The traditional Normandy
recipe calls for a final sprinkling of chopped black
truffle — a decorative and delicious if somewhat
extravagant touch.

SALADE DE RIZ A L'ORIENTALE

ORIENTAL RICE SALAD

Preparation time 20 minutes
To serve 4

You will need

8 oz. long grain rice
salt
4 tablespoons olive oil
1 tablespoon tarragon *or* wine vinegar
2 tomatoes, skinned and chopped
half sweet green pepper, shredded
a few green olives, stoned
4 oz. cooked meat *or* poultry, diced
4 slices honeydew melon (optional)
a few onion rings (optional)

Cook the rice in plenty of fast boiling salted water
until *just* tender, 12—18 minutes depending on
type used. Drain thoroughly. While still hot mix
with the oil and vinegar, prepared tomatoes,
green pepper, olives and cooked meat *or* poultry.
Pile into a salad bowl. When cold impale the melon
slices (if used), on the sides of the bowl. Garnish
with onion rings, if liked.

Oriental rice salad

SALADE NICOISE

SALAD NICE STYLE

(Illustrated in colour opposite)
Preparation time 15 minutes
To serve   3–4

You will need

Vinaigrette dressing (see page 109)
1 lettuce heart, crisped
8 oz. cooked French beans
4 oz. can tunny fish (optional)
2 oz. small black olives
a few stuffed green olives (optional)
thin strips de-seeded green pepper
8 anchovy fillets
a few thin onion rings (optional)
12 oz. firm tomatoes, quartered
2 hard-boiled eggs, quartered

For this there is no exact recipe, ingredients and proportions being varied according to availability. For a typical salad put half dressing in bottom of a shallow bowl and in it toss lettuce leaves and beans. On top arrange small lumps of tunny fish, if used, olives, green pepper, anchovy fillets and onion rings, etc... Surround with quarters of tomato and hard-boiled egg; sprinkle with remaining Vinaigrette. Serve immediately.

Note
Garlic and herbs are often added to the Vinaigrette.

SALADE TOURANGELLE

GREEN BEAN
AND POTATO SALAD

Line a salad bowl with washed and crisped lettuce leaves. Toss 8 oz. cooked diced French beans and 6 oz. cooked, diced potatoes in Vinaigrette à la Crème (see page 109); pile in centre. Garnish with 2 tomatoes, skinned and sliced.

POMMES DE TERRE A L'HUILE

FRENCH POTATO SALAD

Preparation time 25 minutes
To serve   3–4

You will need

1 lb. waxy potatoes
2 tablespoons wine *or* tarragon vinegar
4–5 tablespoons olive oil
salt and pepper to taste
1 tablespoon chopped spring onion (optional)
chopped fresh herbs

Scrub potatoes and boil, in their jackets, in salted water, until *just* tender. Drain, and when cool enough to handle peel and cut into $\frac{1}{4}$-inch slices. Mix vinegar, oil, seasonings and spring onion (if used), together, and toss lightly with the hot potatoes. Served warm or cold, sprinkled with herbs.

SALADE DE TOMATES

TOMATO SALAD

Preparation time 10 minutes
To serve   4

You will need

1 lb. *firm* ripe tomatoes
salt
3 tablespoons olive oil
$\frac{1}{2}$ tablespoon lemon juice *or* wine vinegar
a few slices onion (optional)
chopped fresh parsley *or* chives

Without peeling cut tomatoes crosswise into *thin* slices (use serrated edged knife) and arrange overlapping on a flat dish. Sprinkle with salt, leave to stand for 1 hour. Just before serving drain off extracted water. Mix oil and lemon juice *or* vinegar sprinkle over tomatoes. Sprinkle with a few onion rings (if used), and some chopped parsley or chives.

Salade Niçoise (Salad Nice style)

Les huîtres (Oysters)

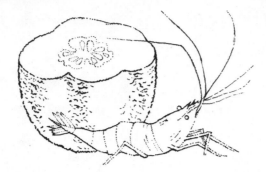

THE COLD TABLE

LES PIECES FROIDES

Cold dishes are particularly useful for summer catering and for buffet parties at any time of the year.

Most of the French cold table recipes in this chapter need time and patience to prepare but will provide classic centre pieces for you table. It is unwise to attempt the aspic dishes unless ice and a refrigerator are available. Simpler cold fare, equally suitable for cold meals, will be found in other parts of the book, in particular in the chapters dealing with Pâtés (page 28) and Salads (page 108).

Many colourful and typically French ideas are given in the Hors-d'oeuvre chapter beginning page 13, for example Accordian Tomatoes, and Mushrooms stewed in oil and wine.

And other cold vegetable ideas will be found in the chapter on vegetables.

POULET EN GELÉE

JELLIED TARRAGON CHICKEN

Preparation time 1 hour
Cooking time 1¼ hours
To serve 4–6

You will need

3 lb. chicken, oven ready
salt
1 oz. butter
8 sprigs fresh tarragon
1 tablespoon oil
1½ oz. powdered gelatine
1½ pints (U.S. 3¾ cups) good chicken stock
 or canned consommé
few drops gravy browning if necessary
4–5 tablespoons Madeira *or* port

Dry the chicken, sprinkle inside liberally with salt and insert a nut of butter and 3 sprigs fresh tarragon. Heat the remaining butter and the oil in a flameproof casserole and brown chicken on all sides, this will take about 12—15 minutes. Cover and cook in pre-heated moderate oven (350°F. or Gas Mark 4), for 1 hour. Remove chicken and set aside until absolutely cold.

Sprinkle the powdered gelatine into the stock *or* consommé and heat gently until dissolved. Add 3 sprigs tarragon, and if necessary a few drops of browning to give the stock a light brown colour. Cover and leave to stand for 15 minutes. Check seasoning, add Madeira *or* port to taste, then strain jelly through several thicknesses of muslin. Pour ⅛-inch layer of jelly into the serving dish and leave to set. Carve the chicken and arrange the pieces on the jelly. Chill remaining jelly and stir over ice until almost set, but still fluid, then spoon over chicken.

Repeat at intervals, as necessary and arrange a decoration of tarragon leaves before the final coating.

Pour the remaining jelly into a shallow tin and when set cut into shapes, or chop, to garnish the edge of the dish.

TRUITE SAUMONÉE EN GELÉE
COLD SALMON TROUT IN ASPIC

Preparation time   3 hours, including cooling
               of aspic
Cooking time   30 minutes
To serve   4–6

You will need

1 salmon trout, 2–3 lb. in weight
salt
FISH ASPIC JELLY
1¼ pints (U.S. 3⅛ cups) fish poaching liquor
¼ pint (U.S. ⅝ cup) dry white wine
2 tablespoons tarragon vinegar
1 small carrot, sliced
1 onion, chopped
whites and shells of 2 eggs
1½ oz. powdered gelatine
slices of cucumber, small tomatoes filled with
    mayonnaise, to garnish

See that gills and intestines of fish have been
removed, scrape away any blood along the back-
bone. Cradle fish in a piece of clean muslin. Fill
a container with water to cover fish and add
1 teaspoon salt per 2 pints (U.S. 5 cups). When
simmering lower fish into water; poach gently
allowing 10 minutes per lb. Allow to cool in water
for 30 minutes then lift out and drain. Carefully
remove skin. Prepare aspic as follows. Place all
ingredients in a saucepan and bring to the boil
whisking with a wire whisk. A thick froth will form
on top. Stand for 15 minutes then pour very gently
through several thicknesses of muslin into a basin.
Leave in a cold place until just beginning to set.
Glaze fish and run a little aspic over serving dish.
When both are set place fish on dish and surround
with remaining set jelly, chopped. Garnish with
cucumber slices and tomatoes filled with mayonnaise. Hand mayonnaise *or* sauce rémoulade (see
page 119) separately.

CORNETS DES SAUCISSES
GARLIC SAUSAGE CORNETS

Preparation time   about 20 minutes
Cooking time   no cooking
To serve   6

You will need

4 oz. thinly sliced large garlic sausage
half a small ripe melon
4–6 oz. peeled prawns
about ⅓ pint (U.S. ⅞ cup) stiff mayonnaise (see
    page 119)
6 whole Mediterranean prawns for garnish
sprigs of parsley

Roll sausage slices into cornet shapes and secure
with cocktail stick. Chop melon into ¼-inch dice
(or form into balls with a *small* ball cutter) and
drain well. Mix with prawns and mayonnaise. Fill
the cornets; arrange on cirucular platter. Garnish
with whole prawns and sprigs of parsley.

BOEUF A LA MODE EN GELÉE
JELLIED BRAISED BEEF

Follow recipe for Beef braised in wine (see page
78), but without thickening liquid. When meat
is soft remove and slice it. Arrange slices overlapping in a deep dish. Surround with freshly
cooked sliced carrots. Strain stock, skim off surplus
fat; check seasoning. Cool a little on a saucer to
see that it jellies; (if not reduce further or add
a little gelatine). Pour stock over meat. When cold
and jellied gently remove surface fat. Serve with
a green salad.

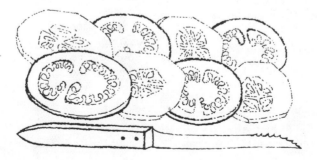

Cornets des saucisses (Garlic sausage cornets)

SAUCES, FLAVOURED BUTTERS

LES SAUCES, LES BEURRES COMPOSÉS

There is sheer genius in the way in which the French transform simple everyday food — such as eggs, white fish, vegetables and even left-overs into dishes of distinction simply by adding an interesting sauce.

Many French sauces are easier to make than most people imagine. Their main requirements are good quality fresh ingredients (you cannot for instance make a good mayonnaise with stale olive oil) and careful attention to detail. The critical points of temperature and consistency have been empha-

sised in the recipes in this chapter, and once you have mastered four basic sauces (Béchamel, Brune, Hollandaise and Mayonnaise) you will have many variations at your command as well.

Keeping a sauce hot is a problem the French solve by means of a water bath, known as a 'bain-marie'. Stand the saucepan containing the sauce in a deep baking tin half filled with hot water. In this way the sauce has gentle heat all round it and will keep for hours. Cover the saucepan with a lid to prevent a skin from forming.

BEURRES COMPOSÉS

FLAVOURED BUTTERS

COLD FLAVOURED BUTTERS

Flavoured butters add finishing touches to plain foods such as grilled meat or fish and boiled vegetables. Also used for spreading on canapés, and for enriching soups.

BEURRE AU CITRON
Cream 2 oz. butter with 2 teaspoons of lemon juice, and salt and pepper.

BEURRE MAÎTRE D'HÔTEL
As above plus 1 tablespoon finely chopped parsley.

BEURRE D'ESCARGOTS
Cream 2 oz. butter with 1 tablespoon grated shallot, 1—2 cloves crushed garlic, 1 tablespoon chopped parsley and seasoning.

BEURRE DE RAIFORT
Cream 2 oz. butter with 1 teaspoon of finely grated fresh horseradish.

BEURRE DE CREVETTES
Pound equal weights of shelled prawns and butter together, add a few drops of carmine, and press through a sieve.

TO MAKE CHILLED BUTTER SHAPES
Form flavoured butter into a 1-inch diameter roll and chill. Cut into slices as required.

HOT FLAVOURED BUTTERS

BEURRE NOISETTE
Heat butter in a frying pan until it begins to turn brown and smell of nuts. Use immediately.

BEURRE NOIR
As above but heated to a deeper colour. Pour over the food immediately then swill out pan with a little wine vinegar and pour this too over the food.

MAYONNAISE

Preparation time 10–15 minutes
Cooking time no cooking
To serve 4

You will need

2 fresh egg yolks
½ level teaspoon salt
¼ level teaspoon dry mustard *or* ½ level
   teaspoon French mustard
½–1 tablespoon wine *or* tarragon vinegar,
   or lemon juice
about ½ pint (U.S. 1¼ cups) oil*

* Use olive, ground nut, corn or a mixture of oils
according to personal taste.

Have all ingredients at *room temperature*. Put egg
yolks in a small pudding basin standing on a folded
damp cloth. Add salt, mustard and a few drops
of vinegar *or* lemon juice and beat thoroughly
before adding any oil. Use a small wire whisk *or*
wooden spoon for mixing. Have the oil in a measuring jug with lip but add *drop by drop* from a teaspoon
to start, *beating all the time*. When the mayonnaise
thickens add half teaspoon of vinegar or lemon
juice and increase the flow of oil to an intermittent
thin stream, *beating continuously*. Continue until all
the oil is added, when the consistency should be
thick and jelly like.
Add a little more lemon juice and seasoning if
wished.

Mayonnaise
Adding the oil from a teaspoon to the well mixed egg
yolk and seasonings

TO THIN A MAYONNAISE beat in a teaspoon or
so of water, thin cream or dry white wine.

TO STIFFEN A MAYONNAISE FOR COATING beat in
a ¼ oz. gelatine dissolved in 2 tablespoons hot
water and use immediately.

TO REMEDY A CURDLED MAYONNAISE add, *very
gradually* at first, to a fresh egg yolk *or* to a heaped
teaspoon of made French mustard, in a clean bowl.

SAUCES MADE WITH MAYONNAISE

MAYONNAISE CHANTILLY

Flavour with lemon juice, and fold in ⅛ pint
(U.S. ⅓ cup) double cream.

SAUCE TARTARE

Add 1 teaspoon *each* grated onion, chopped capers,
gherkins, tarragon and parsley.

SAUCE AIOLI

Pound to a paste 2 peeled cloves garlic in the basin
before adding the egg yolks.

SAUCE NIÇOISE

Add 1 heaped tablespoon *thick* Tomato Coulis,
made from fresh tomatoes (see page 122), ¼ teaspoon paprika pepper and 1 teaspoon chopped
fresh tarragon.

SAUCE RÉMOULADE

Add 1 heaped teaspoon each French mustard,
chopped parsley, chervil, shallot and gherkin.

Mayonnaise
A thick glossy mayonnaise

SAUCE BÉARNAISE

BÉARNAISE SAUCE

Preparation time 10 minutes
Cooking time 10 minutes
To serve 3–4

You will need

4 tablespoons wine vinegar ⎫ *or* 4 tablespoons
large sprig tarragon, chopped ⎰ tarragon vinegar
4 crushed peppercorns
1 teaspoon chopped shallot
3–4 oz. butter, at warm room temperature
2 egg yolks
1 teaspoon each chopped tarragon and parsley

Put the wine vinegar and tarragon *or* tarragon vinegar, peppercorns and shallot into a small saucepan and simmer until only 1 tablespoon liquid remains. Strain through muslin or very fine sieve into a basin resting over a saucepan half filled with warm water. Set pan over *low* heat and to do *not* allow to boil. Add 1 tablespoon cold water and ½ oz. butter to the vinegar reduction. Add beaten egg yolks and whisk with small wire whisk until sauce thickens; then *immediately* begin whisking in the softened butter, about ½ oz. at a time. When all is added, and the sauce thick and creamy, stir in the herbs and adjust seasoning. Serve this sauce *warm*, not hot, as *overheating* at *any time* will cause separation and curdling. Use for beef steaks, fish, chicken and egg dishes.

BEURRE BLANC

BUTTER SAUCE

Preparation time 5 minutes
Cooking time 10 minutes
To serve 3–4

You will need

3 shallots
3 tablespoons wine vinegar
pinch salt and white pepper
4 oz. unsalted butter, at room temperature

A very delicate sauce from the Loire valley. Chop shallots until almost *a purée* then put into a small saucepan with vinegar and seasonings; cook *gently*

Béarnaise sauce
Straining the reduced herb flavoured vinegar into a basin

until shallots are tender and liquid reduced to 1 tablespoonful. Remove from heat and allow to cool. Just before serving hold pan over a *very low* heat (or stand over warm water) and whisk in the butter ½ oz. at a time. The butter must not liquify but emulsify with the shallots to form a cream consistency. Correct seasoning, and serve at once in a barely warm bowl. Use for fresh water fish, sea bass, turbot and salmon dishes.

SAUCE BÉCHAMEL

BASIC WHITE SAUCE

Preparation time 5 minutes
Cooking time 10 minutes
To serve 4

You will need

1¼ oz. butter
1 oz. plain flour
½–¾ pint (U.S. 1¼–1⅞ cups) boiling liquid*
salt and white pepper to taste

* Use smaller quantity for a coating sauce, larger quantity for a medium sauce. The liquid may be all milk, *or* part milk and part vegetable liquor *or* white stock.

Melt the butter in a heavy saucepan over low heat. Add the flour and stir with small wire whisk, cooking the roux gently *without colouring*, for 2—3 minutes. Remove from heat. Add the liquid all at once, whisking vigorously until blended. Bring to the boil, stirring, and simmer over low heat for

Béarnaise sauce
Whisking the butter little by little into thickened sauce

at least 5 minutes, preferably longer. Season and use as required.

VARIATIONS

SAUCE VELOUTÉ

Use concentrated chicken, fish *or* veal stock instead of milk.

SAUCE CRÈME

Add 3—4 tablespoons double cream to the cooked sauce and finish with a few drops lemon juice.

SAUCE MORNAY

Off heat add 1½ oz. grated mixed Parmesan and Swiss cheese, a little grated nutmeg and shake of cayenne pepper.

SAUCE SOUBISE

Boil 8 oz. onions until tender. Drain, chop and sieve. Add to ½ pint (U.S. 1¼ cups) *thick* Béchamel Sauce with 2 tablespoons double cream and a pinch of nutmeg. Adjust seasoning and reheat without boiling.

SAUCE HOLLANDAISE

HOLLANDAISE SAUCE

Preparation time   10 minutes
Cooking time   10 minutes
To serve   3—4

You will need

2 egg yolks
1 tablespoon lemon juice (scant)
1 tablespoon water
pinch each salt and white pepper
4 oz. unsalted butter, at room temperature

Whisk the egg yolks, lemon juice, water and seasoning together in a small basin. Rest the basin over a pan of hot (not boiling) water and whisk steadily until mixture thickens to a cream. Immediately remove from heat and add the butter, ½ oz. at a time, whisking in each addition until completely absorbed. The result should be a creamy sauce of coating consistency. Thin with a few drops of warm water if necessary. Serve tepid and never allow the sauce to overheat. Use for asparagus, fish and egg dishes.

SAUCE BRUNE

BASIC BROWN SAUCE

Preparation time   15 minutes
Cooking time   30 minutes–1 hour
To serve   4

You will need

2 oz. pork *or* beef dripping
2 oz. onion, chopped
3 oz. lean bacon, chopped
stick celery, chopped
1 oz. flour
¾ pint (U.S. 1⅞ cups) stock
1 teaspoon tomato purée
sprig each parsley and thyme, *or* ¼ teaspoon dried
small bay leaf
salt, sugar and pepper to taste

Heat fat in pan; fry onion, bacon and celery for 5 minutes. Add flour, cook, stirring, allowing it *slowly* to turn nut brown. Add stock, tomato purée, herbs and seasonings, whisk until boiling. Cover, *simmer* for 30 minutes — 1 hour or longer, (the longer you cook a brown sauce the finer the flavour), skimming off fat and scum. Press through sieve, reheat; adjust seasoning. Final consistency should coat back of spoon, so if during cooking sauce reduces too much add a little more stock.

VARIATIONS

SAUCE MADÈRE

Add 4 tablespoons Madeira halfway through cooking. Use for ham, beef, veal and egg dishes.

SAUCE PIQUANTE

Fry 2 oz. chopped shallot in 1 oz. butter. Add 1 tablespoon wine vinegar, boil until almost evaporated. Add strained Sauce Brune, 2 oz. chopped gherkins, ¼ teaspoon French mustard, 1 oz. butter. Reheat. Use for pork, boiled beef or leftovers.

OEUFS MAZARINE

EGG CUSTARD WITH TOMATO SAUCE

(Illustrated in colour opposite)
Preparation time 10 minutes
Cooking time 1–1¼ hours
To serve 4

You will need

1 pint (U.S. 2½ cups) milk
5 eggs
pinch grated nutmeg
salt and pepper
1 recipe Tomato Sauce (see below)

Pre-heat oven to (310°F. or Gas Mark 2). Beat the eggs lightly and season with nutmeg, salt and pepper. Heat the milk then add little by little to the eggs, stirring all the time. Strain into a buttered mould, cover, and stand in a baking tin half filled with hot water. Bake until set firm, about 1—1¼ hours. Loosen edges with a knife, and turn out into a shallow dish. Pour the well reduced tomato sauce over the custard and serve soon.

SAUCE TOMATE

TOMATO SAUCE

Preparation time 15 minutes
Cooking time 30–40 minutes
To serve 4

You will need

1 oz. pork *or* bacon fat
1 oz. each chopped onion, carrot and celery
1 rasher streaky bacon, chopped
1 level tablespoon flour
¼ pint (U.S. ⅝ cup) stock *or* water
1¼ lb. ripe tomatoes, quartered
1 clove garlic, crushed
bouquet garni (see page 106)
salt, pepper and sugar to season

Over gentle heat fry the vegetables and bacon in the fat for 5 minutes. Sprinkle in the flour, stir and cook for a minute then add the stock *or* water, tomatoes, garlic, bouquet garni, and seasonings. Bring to the boil, cover, and simmer for 30—40 minutes. Press through a sieve and return to rinsed pan. Adjust consistency as necessary, thinning with extra stock *or* water or concentrating by rapid boiling.
Check seasoning and serve hot.

COULIS DE TOMATES A LA PROVENCALE

FRESH TOMATO PURÉE

Preparation time 10 minutes
Cooking time 20 minutes
To serve 3

You will need

2 oz. chopped onion
1 tablespoon olive oil
1 clove garlic, crushed
1 lb. ripe tomatoes, roughly chopped
¼ teaspoon dried marjoram *or* basil
salt, sugar, and black pepper to taste
½-inch strip orange peel

In a heavy saucepan gently fry the chopped onion in the oil for 5 minutes. Add all the remaining ingredients.
When boiling, cover, and simmer until pulped, for about 20 minutes. Press through a sieve, return the sauce to the rinsed pan, and boil rapidly, stirring frequently, until reduced to a thickish purée. Adjust the seasoning.
Use for egg, chicken, pasta and meat dishes.

Oeufs mazarine (Egg custard with tomato sauce)

Coulibiac de saumon (Russian salmon pie)

SAVOURY PASTRIES, ENTRÉES

LES PATES SALÉES

French cooking abounds in deliciously savoury dishes. Many of these are based on puff or rich shortcrust pastry, always made with butter, and with light, crisp, melt-in-the-mouth textures. Although for speed and convenience many of us often use ready to roll, pastries, when time permits it is always rewarding to practise the arts of traditional pastry making. Puff and rich shortcrust both benefit from 'resting' periods so if more convenient make one day for the next, or in the morning for use in the evening. Typically French gnocchi and pancake recipes have been included in this chapter; they make tasty and economical luncheon or supper dishes. Space had to be found too for Croissant (not strictly a savoury pastry but not exactly a sweet one either) whose appearance on the breakfast table has done so much to reconcile holiday makers to the frugal 'continental' breakfast.

The famous savoury flans, called 'Quiche' or 'Tarte' in French make excellent meal starters, supper or picnic dishes.

COULIBIAC DE SAUMON

RUSSIAN SALMON PIE

(Illustrated in colour opposite)
Preparation time 30 minutes
Cooking time 30–40 minutes
To serve 4

You will need

12 oz. piece salmon, lightly poached
3 oz. butter
2 oz. flour
½ pint (U.S. 1¼ cups) milk
3 oz. shallot *or* onion, finely chopped
4 oz. mushrooms, sliced
2 hard-boiled eggs, chopped
salt and pepper
8 oz. made puff pastry
beaten egg for glazing

This is a French adaptation of a classic Russian recipe.
Cook and cool the salmon. Make a *thick* Béchamel sauce with 1½ oz. of the butter, the flour and the milk (see page 120). Melt the remaining butter in a saucepan and fry the prepared shallot *or* onion and mushrooms very gently for 6—8 minutes. Stir in the sauce, hard-boiled eggs and seasoning to taste. On a sheet of lightly floured greaseproof paper roll out the pastry to a rectangle 12-inches by 9-inches. Spread half the cold sauce along centre of pastry, leaving 3-inch margin all round. Divide salmon into large pieces, discarding skin and bone, and place on sauce. Cover with rest of sauce. Damp edges of pastry, fold ends inwards and sides to overlap in centre, forming a 'bolster'. Using paper turn upside down on to damp baking sheet so that the join is underneath. Brush with beaten egg, and mark criss cross fashion with a knife. Bake in a pre-heated hot oven (425°F. or Gas Mark 7), for 30—40 minutes, until pastry crisp and golden. Serve hot, in thick slices, as a fish course or a meal starter.

Note

The original Russian Coulibiac was usually made with a rich yeast pastry.

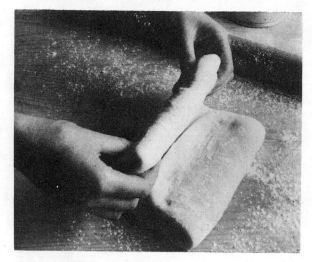

CROISSANTS

CRESCENT ROLLS

Preparation time about 3½ hours or overnight
Cooking time   10–12 minutes
Makes   about 12 croissants

You will need

8 oz. plain flour
1 level teaspoon salt
1 level tablespoon castor sugar
½ oz. yeast
3½ oz. butter (firm 'waxy' type)
¼ pint (U.S. ⅝ cup) *warm* milk
beaten egg and milk to glaze

Croissants, those deliciously light and flaky crescent shaped rolls served in France for breakfast, are surprisingly simple to make. The dough can be refrigerated overnight, then shaped and baked in time for (late) breakfast. Sift the flour, salt and sugar into a mixing bowl and make a 'well' in the centre. Dissolve the yeast in the milk, pour into the 'well' and mix in the flour to form a fairly *soft* dough. Turn onto a floured work surface and knead thoroughly for 4—5 minutes then cover with foil or polythene and leave for 30 minutes or until volume has increased by one third. Roll the dough into a small oblong, flatten the butter with floured rolling pin and place in *centre* of dough (it should cover nearly half the surface) then fold one end of dough up and other end down to meet in the centre. Fold in half like a book and give a quarter turn. * Roll out to be a ¼-inch thick oblong, fold one

end of dough up and other end down to meet, then 'book' fold in half *. Give a quarter turn and roll out in opposite direction. Repeat from * to * once more then wrap *loosely* in foil or polythene and leave at room temperature for 2 hours or overnight in refrigerator. When ready to shape roll out to a rectangle about 11-inches by 18-inches, trim edges and divide in half lengthwise.

Divide each strip into six triangles, each with a 6-inch base. Roll up each triangle from base to tip, moistening the tip with beaten egg to hold it in position. Place on greased and floured baking sheets and form into crescent shapes. Cover and place in a warm place for 15—20 minutes, until well puffed up. Bake towards top of pre-heated hot oven (425°F. or Gas Mark 7), for 7—8 minutes. Brush lightly with beaten egg and return to oven for another 3—4 minutes, until cooked and golden. Cool on a wire tray. Serve warm, with or without butter.

Note
Croissants will keep for several days in an airtight tin but should be warmed in a hot oven to crisp them again before serving.

PATE FEUILLETÉE

PUFF PASTRY

Preparation time 2–3 hours

You will need

8 oz. plain flour
½ level teaspoon salt
8 oz. firm butter, waxy type for preference
Scant ¼ pint (U.S. ⅝ cup) ice cold water

Puff pastry is much used in France for both savoury and sweet and dishes.

The most 'melting' pastry is made with butter, but the use of ready-made or frozen pastry saves several hours of labour. Except in cold weather it is not advisable to make puff pastry without the help of a refrigerator.

Sift flour and salt into a mixing bowl and rub in ½ oz. of butter. Make a hole in centre, add water and mix to a firm but elastic dough. Cover; leave to relax for 20 minutes. Then, on a lightly floured work surface roll pastry into a rectangle, ¼-inch thick. Flatten butter into an oblong a little less than half the size of the pastry. Place butter flat in centre of pastry and fold edges over to meet in centre, forming a parcel. Turn over.* Roll dough into an oblong about 3 times longer than the width, and ¼-inch thick. Fold in three, bringing end nearest you up the strip and folding the far end over towards you, forming a square. Seal edges with rolling pin trapping as much air as possible. Give a quarter turn to left so that pastry is rolled in opposite direction next time.* Repeat from * to * once.

Wrap in foil and refrigerate for 20 minutes.

Repeat this rolling, folding and chilling process until the pastry has had 6 rollings in all. Wrap in foil and refrigerate for 2 hours or until required. The pastry is all the better for resting overnight. Will keep for 2—3 days in refrigerator or deep frozen for up to a month.

GNOCCHI A LA PARISIENNE

GNOCCHI PARIS STYLE

Preparation time 30 minutes
Cooking time about 25 minutes
To serve 3–4

You will need

¼ pint (U.S. ⅝ cup) milk
1½ oz. butter
2½ oz. flour, sifted
2 eggs
2 oz. Gruyère cheese, grated
salt and pepper
grated nutmeg
½ pint (U.S. 1¼ cups) Mornay Sauce
  (see page 121)

Bring milk and butter just to the boil, draw aside and at once add all the flour. Beat until smooth. Beat in the eggs one at a time, 1 oz. of the grated cheese and seasonings of salt, pepper and nutmeg. Prepare a wide saucepan of boiling salted water; remove from heat. Using two large teaspoons drop small balls of paste into the water and poach for 7—8 minutes or until firm. Remove with a perforated spoon, drain on a folded clean tea towel and arrange in a buttered shallow fireproof dish. Coat with well seasoned and not too thick Mornay Sauce, and sprinkle with the remaining grated cheese. Bake in a pre-heated moderate oven (350°F. or Gas Mark 4), for about 15 minutes. Serve quickly while the gnocchi are puffed up and light; if left they subside again.

VOL-AU-VENT

'PUFF OF WIND' PASTRY CASES

A vol-au-vent is a pastry case usually of a size to serve 3—4 people. Make 1 recipe Puff Pastry (or use 1 lb. bought pastry) and roll out on a lightly floured cold surface to ¾-inch thick. Invert a 6 to 7-inch diameter plate, or an oval pie dish, on the pastry. Cut around with a sharp pointed knife held sloping outwards. Place the shape on a damp baking sheet with widest side downwards (this allows for shrinkage during cooking). Brush with beaten egg and score surface lightly with criss-cross knife marks. Half an inch from edge mark an inner shape to form the lid, cutting only half way through the pastry. Bake towards top of pre-heated very hot oven (450°F. or Gas Mark 8), until well risen and golden brown, about 25—30 minutes. Reduce heat and cover pastry with foil if browning too quickly. Remove lid with sharp knife and scoop out soft inner pastry. Return case to oven for a few minutes to dry. Fill with prepared filling and serve hot or warm. Cases can be made in advance and reheated.

BOUCHÉES
INDIVIDUAL PATTIES

Make as vol-au-vent but roll pastry to ½-inch thick and cut cases with a 2½-inch round cutter, traditionally, but not essentially a fluted one. Use a smaller cutter for the lid. Glaze and bake as before, cooking for 15—18 minutes only.

PETITES BOUCHÉES
COCKTAIL PATTIES

As above but using a 1½-inch diameter cutter and baking for 10—12 minutes only.

FILLINGS FOR VOL-AU-VENT AND BOUCHÉES

Heat fillings gently and pile up in warm pastry cases. Set lid askew to show filling and garnish.

PRINCESSE
CHICKEN AND ASPARAGUS

Add 6 oz. chopped cooked chicken meat to ½ pint (U.S. 1¼ cups) Velouté Sauce (see page 121) flavoured with Madeira. Garnish with asparagus tips.

D'OEUFS DURS
HARD-BOILED EGGS IN CHEESE SAUCE

Mix 4 chopped hard-boiled eggs with ½ pint (U.S. 1¼ cups) Mornay Sauce (see page 121).

AUX CREVETTES
SHRIMP

Mix 4 oz. peeled shrimps and 4 oz. cooked sliced mushrooms with ½ pint Béchamel Sauce (U.S. 1¼ cups), (see page 120). Garnish with shrimp heads.

À LA REINE
CHICKEN AND TRUFFLES

Add 6 oz. chopped cooked chicken and 1—2 canned truffles and their juices (1 small can) to ½ pint (U.S. 1¼ cups) Velouté Sauce (see page 121).

MARINIÈRE
MUSSELS

Prepare fresh mussels Marinière Style (see page 56) and mix with a thick cream sauce (see page 121).

SACRISTAINS DE FROMAGE
TWISTED CHEESE BATONS

Preparation time 20 minutes
Cooking time 6–8 minutes
Makes about 30

You will need

6 oz. puff pastry trimmings*
finely grated Parmesan cheese
salt and pepper
few grains cayenne pepper
egg to glaze

* or 6 oz. frozen pastry, just thawed.

Roll pastry out thinly. Sprinkle evenly all over with grated Parmesan seasoned with salt and pepper and a few grains of cayenne. Fold in three, re-roll, and repeat once more.
Finally roll pastry thinly and cut into $3\frac{1}{2}$-inch wide bands. Trim edges neatly. Brush all over with beaten egg and sprinkle with grated cheese. Cut into $\frac{1}{4}$-inch wide finger strips. Take each strip in turn, holding at each end, and twist twice. Place immediately on damp baking sheet pressing ends securely to tray. Bake in a pre-heated very hot oven (450°F. or Gas Mark 8), for 6—8 minutes, until crisp and golden. Serve as cocktail savouries.

ALLUMETTE AUX ANCHOIS
ANCHOVY STICKS

Preparation time 15 minutes
Cooking time 7–10 minutes
Makes about 16

You will need

6 oz. puff pastry or trimmings*
small can anchovy fillets
egg to glaze
few small currants

* or 6 oz. packet frozen pastry, just thawed.

Pre-heat oven to (450°F. or Gas Mark 8). Roll pastry out very thinly into an oblong about 9-inches wide. Cut into bands about $4\frac{1}{2}$-inches wide and trim the edges neatly. Cut into $1\frac{1}{2}$-inch wide fingers and lay 1 anchovy fillet on each. Brush edges with egg and wrap pastry around anchovy, sealing edges, and turning so that join is underneath. Shape one end to resemble a fish's head, using a small currant for the eye. Slit the other end and fan out like a tail. Place on a damp baking sheet and brush with egg. Bake towards top of pre-heated oven for 7—10 minutes until pastry is cooked and golden. Serve hot as an hors-d'oeuvre or with cocktails.

Twisted cheese batons

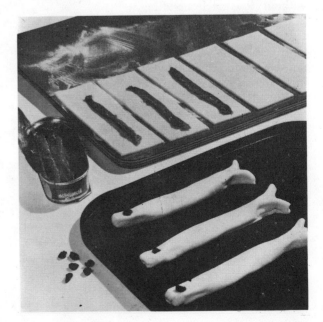

Anchovy sticks

PATE BRISÉE

RICH SHORT FLAN PASTRY

Preparation time 15 minutes

You will need

6 oz. plain flour
pinch salt
1 level teaspoon castor sugar
4 oz. firm butter
1—2 tablespoons cold water

Good French flan pastry is short, tender and buttery. It should be mixed quickly and lightly without too much handling.
Sift flour, salt and sugar into a mixing bowl. Add butter cut in ½-inch pieces and rub lightly into flour with tips of fingers until it resembles oat flakes. (Do not over rub as further blending takes place later). Sprinkle in enough water to bind mixture to a firm but pliable dough. Place on lightly floured board or better still a marble slab. Using the heel of right hand press the pastry, a little at a time, down the board and away from you, making a 'smear' of 6 to 8-inches long. This is known as the 'fraisage' (see illustration above). Gather dough into a ball. Wrap in foil and refrigerate for at least 2 hours before using.
May be kept for 3—4 days in a refrigerator, or deep frozen for one month. This amount of pastry will line an 8-inch flan ring.

QUICHE LORRAINE

CREAM, EGG AND BACON TART

Preparation time 15 minutes
Cooking time 35–40 minutes
To serve 4–5

You will need

1 recipe rich short flan pastry (see opposite)
4 oz. mild streaky bacon
3 eggs *or* 2 eggs plus 2 yolks
½ pint (U.S. 1¼ cups) single cream
salt, pepper and grated nutmeg to season

Pre-heat oven to (400°F. or Gas Mark 6). Line an 8-inch flan ring with the thinly rolled pastry, trim edges and prick base. Line with greaseproof paper and weight with baking beans. Bake towards top of pre-heated oven for 10 minutes; remove beans and cool. Meanwhile prepare filling. Cut bacon rashers into 1-inch strips, cook in a dry frying pan for a minute until the fat runs, then arrange in bottom of flan. Beat eggs lightly, stir in the cream and seasonings; strain over bacon in flan. Transfer immediately to top of oven and cook for 25—30 minutes until quiche is puffed up and golden brown. Serve at once, alone or with salad, French bread and chilled white or rosé wine. May also be served cold.

VARIATIONS

QUICHE AU FROMAGE
CHEESE QUICHE
Follow the above recipe but stir 3—4 oz. grated Gruyère cheese into the egg and cream mixture. The bacon can be omitted or not, as you like.

QUICHE AUX FRUITS DE MER
SHRIMP, CRAB OR LOBSTER QUICHE
Prepare a partially cooked flan case as for Quiche Lorraine. Fry 1 rounded tablespoon finely chopped onion very gently in 1½ oz. butter until soft. Stir in 4 oz. shelled shrimps (*or* boneless crab *or* lobster meat), and 2 tablespoons dry white wine *or* vermouth and cook briskly for 1—2 minutes. When cool stir in 3 eggs beaten with ¼ pint (U.S. ⅝ cup) double cream, 1 level tablespoon tomato purée and seasoning to taste. Pour into flan case and sprinkle with grated cheese. Bake as before.

QUICHE AUX CHAMPIGNONS
MUSHROOM QUICHE
Prepare a partially cooked flan case as for Quiche Lorraine. Fry 1 rounded tablespoon finely chopped

spring onion gently in 1½ oz. butter for 1 minute. Stir in 8 oz. sliced mushrooms. 1 level teaspoon each salt and lemon juice, cover and cook gently for 5 minutes. Uncover and heat rapidly until liquid evaporates. Add 3 eggs beaten with ½ pint (U.S. 1¼ cups) single cream and seasoning to taste. Pour into flan case and bake as before.

PISSALADIÈRE

PROVENÇAL ONION AND ANCHOVY PIE

Preparation time 30 minutes
Cooking time about 40 minutes
To serve 4–5

You will need

1 recipe rich short flan pastry (see page 130)
3 tablespoons olive oil
1 lb. onions, thinly sliced
1 clove garlic, crushed (optional)
2 large ripe tomatoes, skinned
salt and ground black pepper
small can anchovy fillets
few black olives, halved and stoned

Pre-heat oven to (400°F. or Gas Mark 6). Roll out the pastry and line an 8-inch pie plate. Prick

Provençal onion and anchovy pie

the base, line with greaseproof paper and weight with baking beans. Cook for 15 minutes then remove and leave to cool. Meanwhile heat oil in a wide pan and fry the onions very gently, covered, stirring now and then, until soft and golden. This takes about 20 minutes. Add garlic (if used), the tomatoes previously sliced, and seasoning to taste. Cook, stirring frequently until liquid has evaporated and mixture is fairly stiff. Spread in flan case. Criss cross anchovy fillets over the surface and fill spaces with half olives. Sprinkle with a little olive oil and bake in the pre-heated oven for about 20—25 minutes. Serve hot.

Note

Pissaladière is also made with a bread dough base instead of pastry, as in the picture.

TARTE A L'OIGNON

ONION TART

(Illustrated in colour on page 133)
Preparation time 30 minutes
Cooking time 30 minutes
To serve 4–5

You will need

1 recipe rich short flan pastry (see page 130)
1½ lb. onions
1½ oz. butter
1 tablespoon olive oil
2 whole eggs *or* 3 yolks
¼ pint (U.S. ⅝ cup) double cream
salt, pepper and grated nutmeg

Make the pastry and leave to relax. Peel the onions and slice *very* thinly. Heat butter and oil in a wide pan and cook the onions very gently, covered, stirring now and then. This will take 20—30 minutes. Roll out the pastry thinly and line an 8-inch flan ring. When onions are cooked, off the heat add the eggs and cream well beaten together, and seasoning to taste. Pour into the flan. Cook in centre of pre-heated moderately hot oven (400°F. or Gas Mark 6), for 20 minutes, then reduce heat to (350°F. or Gas Mark 4), for another 10 minutes, or until lightly set. Serve hot. A little grated Gruyère cheese or a few pieces of fried streaky bacon are sometimes added to the filling before the tart is cooked.

LES CRÊPES FARCIES
AU JAMBON

PANCAKES FILLED WITH
HAM AND MUSHROOMS

Preparation time 30 minutes plus resting time
for batter
Cooking time about 30 minutes
To serve 4

You will need

BATTER
4 oz. plain flour
¼ teaspoon salt
2 eggs
1 tablespoon oil
scant ½ pint (U.S. 1¼ cups) milk
FILLING
½ pint (U.S. 1¼ cups) thick Béchamel Sauce
(see page 120)
1 oz. butter
1 shallot, finely chopped
4 oz. mushrooms, thinly sliced
salt and pepper
1 level tablespoon chopped parsley
8 *thin* slices of cooked ham
a little single cream
2 level tablespoons grated Parmesan cheese

Sift flour and salt into a bowl. Make a well in
centre and drop in eggs and oil. Add milk gradually, beating continuously with small wire whisk
until a smooth batter of thin cream consistency is
formed. Cover and stand in cool place for 1—2
hours. Make Béchamel Sauce, cover with wet
greaseproof paper and set aside.
Prepare filling as follows. Melt butter and fry
shallot for 1 minute, then add mushrooms and
seasoning; cover pan and cook gently for 3—4
minutes. Add parsley and 3 tablespoons of Béchamel Sauce. Keep warm. Cook the pancakes in the
usual way. When all are cooked, lay a thin slice

of ham on each, spread a spoonful of filling in the
centre and roll up. Arrange side by side in shallow
ovenproof dish and coat with remaining sauce
thinned with cream. Sprinkle with cheese and
brown lightly under the grill. Serve hot.

LA GOUGÈRE

A CHEESE RING
FROM BURGUNDY

Preparation time 20 minutes
Cooking time 30—40 minutes
To serve 5—6

You will need

½ pint (U.S. 1¼ cups) milk
2 oz. butter
1 level teaspoon salt
4½ oz. plain flour, sifted
4 standard eggs
3—4 oz. Gruyère cheese, in ¼-inch dice

Pre-heat an oven to moderately hot (375°F. or
Gas Mark 5). Grease a baking sheet. Heat the
milk with the butter and salt until just boiling.
Add the flour all at once and stir and cook for
1—2 minutes until a smooth paste. Off the heat
add the eggs one at a time, beating until smooth
after each addition. Stir in two-thirds of the diced
cheese. On the baking sheet place overlapping
tablespoonsful of the mixture to form a circle
7-inches in diameter with a space in the centre.
Brush with milk and stud top and sides with remaining cheese dice. Bake in centre of pre-heated
oven until well risen and sides of ring are dry and
firm, about 40—50 minutes. Turn off heat and
leave in oven another 5 minutes. (Unless well
cooked and dried the gougère will collapse when
taken from oven.) Serve hot, as a first course or
snack, with a glass of robust red Burgundy.

Tarte à l'oignon (Onion tart)

Gâteau aux marrons (Chestnut gâteau)

SWEETS AND ICES

LES DESSERTS

Nowadays fresh fruit after the cheese is almost routine at French family meals, but on Sundays and special occasions a sweet is served. Such days are especially popular as the sweets are invariably a rather special treat.

The French housewife buys many of her sweets from a local pâtissier — iced gâteaux, cream filled pastries, savarins and so on. Colourful open 'tartes' in great variety are also favourite sweets — square, oblong, round or individual, with a rich short crust or puff pastry case. The filling may be fresh strawberries or cherries, dried prunes and apricots, or raw fruit such as plums, apples and apricots, cooked in the tart. The fruit is attractively glazed

and raw fruit is sometimes bedded in a creamy crème pâtissière (see page 140). Soufflés, mousses, custards and creams are all typically French. They are not difficult to make but seldom in the budget category for their delicate flavour and texture depend on lashings of eggs and cream and often generous doses of liqueurs. But well worth it for the infinite pleasure and satisfaction of producing a luxurious restaurant sweet at a *fraction* of restaurant prices.

Sweets come *after* the cheese in a French meal and if a wine is served it should be a sweet white wine such as a Sauternes, Barsac or perhaps a Quart de Chaume from the Loire.

PETITS POTS DE CREME

LITTLE POTS OF CUSTARD

Preparation time 5 minutes
Cooking time 20–25 minutes
To serve 4

You will need

3 egg yolks
1½ oz. castor sugar
¾ pint (U.S. 1⅞ cups) milk
vanilla flavouring

Beat egg yolks, sugar and vanilla together in a basin then stir in the near boiling milk. Strain into

4 individual cocottes (see page 10). Stand in a roasting tin filled with hot water to reach halfway up the pots. Cover tin with a baking sheet and cook in a pre-heated slow oven (310°F. or Gas Mark 2), until lightly set, 20—25 minutes. Serve cold, as they are or topped with whipped sweetened cream.

VARIATIONS

PETITS POTS DE CRÈME AU CHOCOLAT

LITTLE POTS OF CUSTARD WITH CHOCOLATE

Dissolve 2 oz. plain dessert chocolate in the milk.

PETITS POTS DE CRÈME AU CAFÉ

LITTLE POTS OF CUSTARD WITH COFFEE

Dissolve 1 level dessertspoon instant coffee in the milk.

French apple tart

PROFITEROLES AU CHOCOLAT

CHOUX PUFFS WITH
HOT CHOCOLATE SAUCE

Preparation time   10 minutes
Cooking time   15–20 minutes
To serve   4

You will need

1 recipe Choux Pastry (see page 148)
FILLING
¼ pint (U.S. ⅝ cup) whipped sweetened double
    cream *or* chocolate Crème Pâtissière
    (see page 140)

DARK CHOCOLATE SAUCE
4 oz. plain dessert chocolate
1½ oz. sugar
2 level teaspoons cocoa powder
½ pint (U.S. 1¼ cups) water
2 level teaspoons cornflour

Make the choux pastry and place in teaspoonfuls
about 2-inches apart on a lightly greased baking
tray. Bake in a pre-heated hot oven (400°F. or Gas
Mark 6), for 15—20 minutes, until puffed, golden
and *quite* firm. Cool on a wire.
When cold fill with cream *or* chocolate Crème Pâtissière and pile in a dish.
Just before serving pour the chocolate sauce, hot,
over the puffs.

DARK CHOCOLATE SAUCE
Put broken up chocolate, sugar, cocoa and water
into a saucepan and heat and stir until dissolved.
Simmer 10 minutes or until syrupy then stir in

cornflour blended with a tablespoon of cold water.
Stir and boil for 2 minutes.

TARTE AUX POMMES

FRENCH APPLE TART

Preparation time   30 minutes
Cooking time   25–30 minutes
To serve   4–6

You will need

2 lb. cooking apples
3–4 oz. sugar
1 oz. butter
finely grated rind small orange
1 recipe sweet flan pastry (see page 137)
GLAZE
2 tablespoons each apricot jam and water
1 teaspoon lemon juice

Reserve 2 apples for decorating the top. Peel, core
and cook the remainder, with 2 tablespoons water,
in a covered pan, until tender. Add the sugar,
butter and orange rind and cook uncovered until
reduced to a thick purée. Cool. Roll out pastry
and line an 8-inch flan ring. Fill with cold apple
purée and arrange reserved apples, peeled, cored

Choux puffs with hot chocolate sauce

and *thinly* sliced, over the surface. Bake in a pre-heated moderately hot oven (400°F. or Gas Mark 6), for 25—30 minutes until pastry is cooked and apples tinged brown. Heat the jam, water and lemon juice until syrupy, press through a sieve and spoon glaze over tart. This tart is delicious hot or cold.

PÂTE SUCRÉE

SWEET FLAN PASTRY

Preparation time 15 minutes plus 1 hours resting

You will need

6 oz. plain flour
3 oz. butter at warm room temperature
2 level tablespoons castor sugar
1 egg *or* 2 yolks
1 tablespoon cold water

Sift flour on to a clean cold surface. Make hole in centre and in it put the butter, sugar and egg *or* yolks. Using fingers of one hand, work these three ingredients together until blended. Draw in the flour with a palette knife and continue working lightly, adding a few drops of cold water as necessary to form a smooth dough. Wrap and leave in a cold place for at least an hour.
This pastry can be made in advance and refrigerated until needed.

Ingredients for sweet flan pastry

COMPOTE D'ABRICOTS

STEWED FRESH APRICOTS

Preparation time 10 minutes
Cooking time 10 minutes
To serve 4

You will need

1½ lb. fresh large apricots, washed
6 oz. sugar
½ pint (U.S. 1¼ cups) water
1 teaspoon lemon juice
1 tablespoon Kirsch *or* Cointreau (optional)

Halve apricots, reserve stones. Dissolve sugar in water, boil for 2 minutes. Add apricots, cover; poach until tender, 8—10 minutes.
Remove fruit with a perforated spoon, arrange in a shallow dish. Boil syrup uncovered until syrupy, then add lemon juice, and liqueur. Pour over fruit. Meanwhile crack stones and scatter chopped kernels over the fruit. Serve cold.

Note
Small apricots can be cooked whole and sprinkled with shredded blanched almonds.

TARTE AUX FRAISES

FRESH STRAWBERRY FLAN

Preparation time 15 minutes
Cooking time 25 minutes
To serve 5–6

You will need

8-inch baked flan case
1 recipe Crème Pâtissière (see page 140)
1–2 tablespoons Cointreau *or* Kirsch (optional)
8–12 oz. firm ripe strawberries, hulled
2 heaped tablespoons redcurrant jelly
1 tablespoon water

Make and bake the flan case using sweet flan pastry (see opposite). Make Crème Pâtissière and flavour with the liqueur (if used). Shortly before serving cover base of flan with thick layer of cold Crème Pâtissière and arrange strawberries to cover the surface. Boil jelly and water together and when syrupy spoon glaze over strawberries.

BOULES DE NEIGE SUR CHOCOLATE

SNOWBALLS ON CHOCOLATE

Preparation time 15 minutes
Cooking time   12–15 minutes
To serve   4

You will need

CHOCOLATE CUSTARD
3 oz. dessert block plain chocolate
¾ pint (U.S. 1⅞ cups) milk
4 egg yolks
2 oz. castor sugar
1 level teaspoon cornflour
SNOWBALLS
2 egg whites
2 oz. sifted castor sugar

An enchanting sweet for children. Break up chocolate and dissolve in the milk. Beat egg yolks, sugar and cornflour together in a basin until creamy. Little by little whisk in hot chocolate milk. Return to rinsed pan and heat slowly, stirring continuously, until custard coats back of spoon. Do *not* boil. Strain into a shallow dish and leave to cool. Meanwhile make snowballs. Boil 2-inches of water in a wide pan; remove from the heat. Whisk egg whites until very stiff then fold in sugar. Shaping with 2 soup spoons drop 4 'balls' of egg white mixture into water and poach for 1—2 minutes. Turn over, and when firm but elastic, 1—2 minutes, remove and drain on folded kitchen paper. When cold

arrange the snowballs on the custard and decorate with coarsely grated chocolate.

SAVARIN CHANTILLY

TIPSY CAKE

Preparation time about 2 hours, including
                  rising of dough
Cooking time   about 20 minutes
To serve   4—5

You will need

BASIC SAVARIN
4½ oz. plain flour
¼ oz. fresh yeast
4 tablespoons tepid milk
2 standard eggs
1½ oz. softened butter
1 level teaspoon castor sugar
pinch salt
SYRUP
4 oz. granulated sugar
¼ pint (U.S. ⅝ cup) water
2–3 tablespoons rum *or* Kirsch
GLAZE (optional)
3 tablespoons sieved apricot jam
1 tablespoon water
DECORATION
¼ pint (U.S. ⅝ cup) whipped sweetened
  double cream
candied *or* canned fruit

This is a quick practical chef method for making savarin. Sift flour into warm mixing bowl and make a 'well' in the centre. Dissolve yeast in warm milk, add lightly beaten eggs, and pour into flour. With one hand mix until smooth (the mixture is a soft and sticky one) then beat thoroughly for 4—5 minutes. Cover basin and set to rise in a warm place for 40 minutes or until doubled in bulk. Meanwhile well grease a 7-inch ring mould. When dough is risen add the butter, sugar and salt and beat by hand for 4—5 minutes. Turn into prepared tin, cover, and leave to prove for 15 minutes or till mixture rises to top of tin. Bake the savarin towards top of a pre-heated moderately hot oven (400°F. or Gas Mark 6), for about 20 minutes until firm and brown. To make syrup dissolve sugar in water then simmer for 3 minutes; add flavouring. Turn baked savarin upside down on a wire tray, after

Surprise omelette

5 minutes loosen with a knife and turn into a shallow serving dish. Immediately spoon over the warm syrup, little by little, until sponge is moist throughout and syrup absorbed. To make the glaze (if used) heat and stir sieved apricot jam and water together until smooth then with a pastry brush paint liberally over the sponge. When cold, and shortly before serving, pile whipped cream in centre of savarin and decorate with candied, *or* drained canned fruits.

OMELETTE EN SURPRISE

SURPRISE OMELETTE

Preparation time 10 minutes
Cooking time 2–3 minutes
To serve 5–6 portions

You will need

12 sponge finger biscuits *or* 6–7-inch square
   of sponge cake
2 tablespoons liqueur *or* fruit juice
3 egg whites
4 oz. castor sugar
family size brick of hard ice cream
small can of sliced peaches, drained
castor sugar for dusting

Pre-heat an oven to very hot (450°F. or Gas Mark 8). Arrange the biscuits side by side, or place the sponge, on a flat ovenproof dish. Sprinkle with the liqueur *or* fruit juice. Whisk the egg whites until very stiff and dry, add half the sugar and whisk

until again stiff, then gently fold in the remaining sugar. Fill into a piping bag fitted with a large star pipe. Place the ice cream brick on the sponge base, surround and top with peach slices. Pipe the meringue *to cover completely* the ice cream and peaches. Sprinkle with sugar and put into the hot oven until the meringue is crisp and tinged with gold, about 2—3 minutes. Serve immediately.

CRÊPES SUZETTE

PANCAKES SUZETTE

Preparation time 15 minutes plus 1 hour to
                    stand batter
Cooking time 30 minutes
To serve 4

You will need

BATTER
4 oz. plain flour
1 level tablespoon castor sugar
1 egg and 1 yolk
½ pint (U.S. 1¼ cups) milk and water mixed
1 tablespoon melted butter *or* oil
1 tablespoon brandy
SUZETTE BUTTER
3 oz. unsalted butter
3 oz. castor sugar
finely grated rind 1 large orange
2 tablespoons Grand Marnier *or* Cointreau
TO FLAME
2–3 tablespoons brandy *or* liqueur

A simple version of a spectacular sweet.
Make pancake batter with flour, sugar, eggs and milk and water. Leave to stand for 1—2 hours; just before using stir in butter *or* oil, and brandy. Cook *wafer thin* pancakes in a small frying pan filmed with butter. Stack one on top of the other, leave covered.
Make Suzette Butter by creaming together butter, sugar and rind, then working in liqueur. Spread each pancake with this butter and roll up. Arrange side by side in ovenproof dish, sprinkle with sugar. Heat through in *hot* oven, 5—8 minutes. At table pour brandy *or* liqueur into heated spoon, ignite and pour flaming over the pancakes.

OMELETTE SOUFFLÉ AUX LIQUEURS

LIQUEUR FLAVOURED SOUFFLÉ OMELETTE

Preparation time 5 minutes
Cooking time 2–3 minutes
To serve 2

You will need

3 eggs, separated
2 oz. castor sugar
finely grated rind ½ orange
2 tablespoons liqueur (Grand Marnier,
   Cointreau, apricot brandy, etc.)
½ oz. butter
castor sugar for dusting

A quickly made and dreamy sweet when you don't mind a little last minute cooking. Make in a 10-inch omelette pan *or* make 2 omelettes in a 7-inch pan. Beat egg yolks, sugar, rind and liqueur together until pale and creamy. Start heating omelette pan gently. Whisk egg whites until very stiff, then fold lightly, but not too thoroughly, into the yolks. Heat butter in pan and when foaming pour in the mixture and spread evenly. Cook over *moderate* heat for 1–1½ minutes, then slip under a pre-heated moderate grill and cook another minute until lightly set. Slide on to a hot dish, folding in half as you do so.
Sprinkle with sugar and serve quickly.

VARIATION
OMELETTE AU CONFITURE
JAM SOUFFLÉ OMELETTE

Omit liqueur and fill omelette with 1–2 tablespoons warm apricot jam flavoured with rum.

CRÈME PÂTISSIERE

CUSTARD CREAM FILLING

Preparation time 20 minutes

You will need

2 egg yolks
2 oz. castor sugar
1 oz. plain flour, sifted
½ pint (U.S. 1¼ cups) milk

With small wire whisk beat egg yolks and sugar until pale and thick then work in the flour and 1 tablespoon of milk. Bring remaining milk to boil, and whisk into egg mixture. Return all to pan and whisk until boiling, then cook 2–3 minutes, still whisking. Flavour to taste with vanilla, liqueur, praliné paste (see page 146) *or* 2 oz. melted dessert chocolate.
When cold this cream is used beneath fruit in flans and tartlets and for filling pastries. It is sometimes enriched by the addition of a little butter, and sometimes lightened by adding a stiffly beaten egg white, when it becomes a Crème St. Honoré.

MERINGUES AUX NOISETTES

MERINGUES WITH TOASTED NUTS

Preparation time 10 minutes
Cooking time 1½–2 hours
To serve 4

You will need

2 egg whites .
4 oz. castor sugar, dry and sifted
vanilla flavouring
6 tablespoons double cream
1 oz. flaked almonds, toasted

Whisk egg whites until very stiff and dry. Shake in half the sugar and whisk until again very stiff.

Meringues with toasted nuts

Fold in remaining sugar. Shaping with two dessert-spoons place ovals of mixture on a baking sheet lined with lightly oiled greaseproof paper. Dry out in a very cool oven (240°F. or Gas Mark ¼), for 1½—2 hours. When cold sandwich in pairs with stiffly whisked vanilla flavoured cream and sprinkle with toasted nuts.

VARIATION

BOMBE FAVOURITE

Into ¼ pint (U.S. ⅝ cup) lightly whipped double cream fold 2 level tablespoons castor sugar, 1 tablespoon Kirsch, and 4 broken meringue shells. Pack into mould, freeze as for ice cream. Unmould, and pour sweetened raspberry purée around.

SOUFFLÉ AU GRAND MARNIER
ORANGE LIQUEUR SOUFFLÉ

Preparation time 15 minutes
Cooking time 25–30 minutes
To serve 4–5

You will need

½ pint (U.S. 1¼ cups) less 3 tablespoons milk
strip each orange and lemon rind
2½ oz. sugar
1 oz. flour
¾ oz. butter
4 egg yolks
4 tablespoons Grand Marnier *or* Curaçao
5 egg whites
little icing sugar

Butter a 2-pint soufflé case; pre-heat oven to (350°F. or Gas Mark 4). Reserve two tablespoons of milk. Bring remainder *slowly* to boil with rinds and sugar; remove from heat and infuse for 10 minutes. Blend flour with reserved milk, stir in strained flavoured milk. Bring to boil, stirring continuously, boil for 2 minutes forming a smooth *thick* paste. Off heat stir in butter, egg yolks one by one and liqueur. Whisk egg whites until stiff, fold into mixture in two instalments. Pour into soufflé case, bake in centre of oven 25—30 minutes. Dust surface with icing sugar and leave in oven another 5 minutes. Serve *immediately*.

GATEÂU AUX MARRONS
CHESTNUT GÂTEAU

(Illustrated in colour on page 134)
Preparation time 15 minutes
Cooking time about 40 minutes
To serve 6–8 portions

You will need

GÂTEAU MOUSSELINE
3 eggs, separated
4 oz. castor sugar
2 oz. plain cake flour
1 oz. cornflour
1 level teaspoon baking powder
FILLING
8 oz. can sweetened chestnut purée
2 oz. softened butter
SOFT CHOCOLATE ICING
see below
DECORATION
few marrons glacé (optional)

Pre-heat oven to (350°F. or Gas Mark 4). Line bottom of 6—7-inch round cake tin with grease-proof paper and butter and flour the sides. Put egg yolks into a mixing bowl, add sugar gradually, beating until mixture is pale and mousse like. Sift flour, cornflour and baking powder together *twice*. Whisk the egg whites until very stiff. Using a metal spoon *very delicately* fold in the flour and egg white alternately, adding each in 3 instalments. Bake in prepared tin in centre of oven for about 40 minutes, until springy when touched. Cool on a wire tray. Cream chestnut purée and butter together for the filling. When cold, slice sponge into three and sandwich together with the filling. Prepare chocolate icing and pour over cake, spreading over top and sides. Decorate with marrons glacé.

GLACAGE AU CHOCOLAT
SOFT CHOCOLATE ICING

Put 3 oz. plain dessert chocolate, broken up and 1 tablespoon coffee *or* rum into a small basin resting over a pan of hot water. Stir until melted and smooth. Remove from the heat and beat in 2 oz. unsalted butter, little by little. Use as soon as the icing has cooled to a spreading consistency.

GLACÉ A LA VANILLE

CUSTARD CREAM ICE

Preparation time 15 minutes plus cooling time
Freezing time 1½–2 hours
To serve 4

You will need

4 egg yolks
4 oz. castor sugar
vanilla flavouring
¼ pint (U.S. ⅝ cup) milk
½ pint (U.S. 1¼ cups) single cream

Set refrigerator to coldest setting. Beat egg yolks, sugar and vanilla with wooden spoon until pale and creamy. Heat milk and cream almost to boiling point, stir gradually into egg mixture. Cook in top of double boiler, stirring constantly, until custard thickens to coat back of spoon. Cool, stirring frequently. When cold pour into chilled ice tray and freeze in ice compartment until firm around edges, about 30 minutes. Turn out, whisk vigorously. Return to tray and continue freezing until firm. Turn refrigerator to normal setting and allow ice to 'ripen' before serving.

VARIATIONS

MOUSSE AU KIRSCH

KIRSCH ICE CREAM

Add 2 tablespoons Kirsch to above before freezing. Serve well whipped and semi-frozen, in wine glasses.

GLACÉ PLOMBIÈRE

CANDIED FRUIT ICE

Chop 2 oz. candied fruits (pineapple, cherries, angelica, etc.) and soak in 2 tablespoons of Kirsch *or* Cointreau for 1 hour. Fold into vanilla ice when latter is semi-frozen.

GLACÉ AUX FRAISES

STRAWBERRY CREAM ICE

Preparation time 15 minutes
Freezing time about 2 hours
To serve 3–4

You will need

8 oz. ripe strawberries (fresh *or* frozen)
2 teaspoons lemon juice
2–3 oz. icing sugar
¼ pint (U.S. ⅝ cup) double cream

A rich creamy ice very suitable for making in a domestic refrigerator set at coldest setting. Purée the fruit, stir in lemon juice and enough sugar to sweeten rather well. Whisk cream until thick then lightly fold in the purée. When evenly mixed pour into ice cube tray or a 1-pint mould, cover, and freeze in ice compartment until firm, about 2 hours. Turn refrigerator to normal setting and leave ice to ripen for several hours.

BOMBE ALHAMBRA

(Illustrated in colour opposite)

Prepare 1 recipe vanilla ice cream and freeze until partially frozen. Chill a 2-pint basin and line with the semi-frozen cream ice, pressing it firmly to sides and bottom; freeze until firm. Prepare 1 recipe strawberry cream ice and fill into centre of vanilla lined basin; cover and continue freezing until firm right through. To serve unmould and decorate with whipped cream and fresh strawberries soaked in Kirsch or Cointreau liqueur.

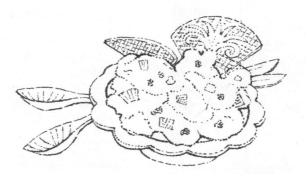

Bombe Alhambra (Strawberry and vanilla cream ice bombe)

Galette Bretonne (Breton flat cake)

PASTRIES AND BISCUITS

LA PÂTISSERIE

In France you won't find the English type of cut-and-come again cakes designed to last the family for several days. Instead you will find pastry shops laden with a wonderful selection of sponges with rich fillings and soft icings, airy confections of puff and choux pastry, groups of dainty petits fours and biscuits, and meringues in various guises. Lending gay splashes of colour there will be open fruit tarts and tartlets in numerous shapes and sizes.

The majority of these confections are intended for eating fresh and are more likely to be served for 'pudding' than with afternoon tea. ('Le thé' is however rapidly becoming a fashionable pastime in French cities.)

Although most Frenchwomen buy their cakes and pastries from a local pâtissier the recipes in this chapter are within the scope of keen home cooks.

But please don't look for economical recipes because generous quantities of eggs, butter and cream are *essential* foundations of genuine French pâtisserie. Expensive, yes, but rich and good.

GALETTE BRETONNE

BRETON FLAT CAKE

(Illustrated in colour opposite)
Preparation time 15 minutes
Cooking time 35–45 minutes
To serve 6 portions

You will need

5 oz. plain flour
pinch salt
3 oz. castor sugar
1 dessertspoon orange flower water
2 large egg yolks
3½ oz. butter at warm room temperature

Sift flour and salt onto a work surface and form into a circle with space in the centre. Into the space put sugar, orange flower water and egg yolks, reserving a small teaspoon of yolk for glazing. Cut butter into pieces and leave on one side.

With fingers of right hand, work sugar and egg yolks together until well mixed. Add butter and continue working, gradually drawing in the flour until a dough is formed.

Handle as little as possible, kneading only until the dough is free from cracks.

Wrap in foil and chill for an hour. Put in centre of a 7-inch flan ring and with knuckles press out to sides of ring. Smooth surface and brush with reserved egg yolk mixed with a teaspoon of water. Mark lightly with a fork.

Bake in the centre of a pre-heated moderate oven (350°F. or Gas Mark 4), for 35—45 minutes, until deep golden brown and cooked through.

This galette, traditional throughout Brittany, has rather a coarse texture and a rich buttery flavour.

PRALINÉ

PRALINÉ FLAVOURING PASTE

You will need

2 oz. unblanched almonds *or* hazel nuts
2½ oz. castor sugar
2 tablespoons water

Spread nuts on baking sheet and 'toast' in a pre-heated moderate oven (350°F. or Gas Mark 4), for 10 minutes. Heat the sugar and water gently in a strong saucepan until dissolved, then boil until caramelised. Immediately stir in toasted nuts and mix thoroughly. Pour on to marble slab or oiled baking sheet.
When cold, break hardened mass into pieces. Pulverise in an electric blender or crush with a rolling pin, then pound with rolling pin (or in pestle and mortar) until a paste is formed.
Use as required and store surplus in screw top jar.

CRÈME AU BEURRE MÉNAGÈRE

BUTTER CREAM

You will need

1 egg yolk
2 oz. sifted icing sugar
3 oz. unsalted butter
FLAVOURING
1 tablespoon rum *or* Kirsch
  or 1 tablespoon orange liqueur
  or 1 tablespoon strong coffee
  or 1 oz. melted plain chocolate
  or praliné flavouring paste (see above)

Put the egg yolk, icing sugar, slightly softened butter and chosen flavouring into a warm dry bowl. Beat until smooth and creamy. If necessary chill until malleable, then use as required to fill or ice cakes.
This icing is not too sweet and may be preferred to other butter creams.

MILLE FEUILLES

THOUSAND LEAF PASTRIES

Preparation time 15 minutes
Cooking time 10–15 minutes
To serve 6–8 portions

You will need

6 oz. puff pastry*
raspberry jam
¼ pint (U.S. ⅝ cup) Crème Chantilly (see page 147)
sifted icing sugar for dusting

* if frozen allow just to thaw.

Pre-heat oven to hot (425°F. or Gas Mark 7). Roll pastry into one large very thin sheet about 12-inches by 11-inches. Place on damp baking sheet, prick well with fork and bake in upper part of pre-heated oven until golden and crisp, about 10—15 minutes. When cold trim edges and cut into 3 even strips about 4-inches wide. Sandwich strips together spreading one layer with jam and other with cream. Press gently but firmly together. Dust heavily with icing sugar and cut into 6—8 slices. Use a saw edged knife for cutting.

PALMIERS GLACÉS

GOLDEN PALM LEAVES

Preparation time 10 minutes
Cooking time 10–12 minutes
To serve makes 15—18 biscuits

You will need

6 oz. puff pastry*
granulated sugar

* trimmings can be used.

Pre-heat an oven to very hot (450°F. or Gas Mark 8). Roll pastry thinly into an oblong, using sugar instead of flour to dust the board. Sprinkle pastry liberally with sugar, fold in three, give a half turn and roll to an oblong 12-inches by 9-inches. Trim edges. Fold opposite shorter sides to the centre so that edges almost meet. Turn one fold over the other, 'book' fashion, and press firmly. Cut across folds into ⅓-inch wide strips. Place on damp baking sheet, cut edges downwards, leaving room for spreading. Bake near top of oven for

10—12 minutes, turning once after 8 minutes or when under side is lightly caramelised. These crisp golden biscuits are delicious alone or with wine or ice cream. You can make palmiers larger or smaller as you wish.

Whisk cream with a wire whisk until it thickens. Add sugar and vanilla flavouring and continue whisking until cream will hold its shape.

CRÈME CHANTILLY

¼ pint (U.S. ⅝ cups) double cream
1—2 teaspoons castor sugar
vanilla flavouring

Golden palm leaves
The baked biscuits — crisp, golden and lightly caramelised

TUILES AUX AMANDES

ALMOND 'TILES'

Preparation time 10 minutes
Cooking time 6–8 minutes
To serve makes 24—30 biscuits

You will need

2 oz. butter
3 oz. castor sugar
1½ oz. plain cake flour, sifted
1 oz. almonds, finely chopped
2 egg whites

Pre-heat oven to moderate (400°F. or Gas Mark 6). Warm a mixing bowl; cream butter and sugar until very soft, white and creamy. Add flour, almonds and stiffly whisked egg whites, and fold in lightly but thoroughly with a metal spoon. Place teaspoonfuls of mixture on greased baking sheets and spread each *thinly* to an oval 2½-inches long. Bake in centre of oven for 6—8 minutes until *just* coloured. Remove as soon as possible from trays and press over a rolling pin to 'curl' before the biscuits become too brittle. These crisp fragile wafers soon soften so store in airtight tin as soon as cool. Serve with ice cream or with a glass of wine.

PÂTE A CHOUX
CHOUX PASTRY

You will need

¼ pint (U.S. ⅝ cup) cold water
1½ oz. butter, cut in pieces
pinch salt
2½ oz. plain flour, sifted and dry
2 standard eggs

Bring the water, butter and salt just to the boil. Draw aside, add the flour all at once, stirring with a wooden spoon. Stir over low heat until mixture forms a smooth ball, in about one minute. Cool a little then beat in the eggs one at a time, until thoroughly and smoothly mixed. The paste should be *just* stiff enough to support the spoon upright, and will look 'shiny'. At this stage the mixture can be set aside for cooking later in the day.

For Cream Choux Buns using a ½-inch diameter pipe form 2-inch choux 'balls' on damp baking tray. Bake as for Paris-Brest (see **opposite**) about 30 minutes. When cold fill with Crème Chantilly (see page 147) and dust thickly with icing sugar.

LES PETITS RELIGIEUSES
LITTLE NUNS

Make up 1 recipe choux pastry (see above). Fill a forcing bag fitted with a ½-inch plain pipe. Onto a damp baking sheet pipe 10 choux 'balls' 1½-inches in diameter and 10 ½-inch in diameter. Bake in a pre-heated oven (400°F. or Gas Mark 6), for 25—30 minutes. When cold fill with vanilla, chocolate *or* coffee flavoured Crème Pâtissière (see

page 140). Ice the large choux 'balls' with chocolate flavoured icing and the small choux 'balls' with coffee icing. Place small choux on top of larger and decorate with tapering 'flames' of coffee butter cream (see page 146).

GÂTEAU PARIS-BREST
PARIS-BREST CHOUX CIRCLE

Preparation time 30 minutes
Cooking time 35–45 minutes
To serve 4

You will need

1 recipe Choux pastry (see opposite)
little beaten egg
1 oz. flaked almonds
Crème Pâtissière (see page 140)
Praliné (see page 146)
1 oz. butter, softened
icing sugar for dusting

Pre-heat oven to (400°F. or Gas Mark 6). Prepare choux pastry and fill a large forcing bag with no pipe affixed (unless a 1-inch pipe is available). Onto a damp baking sheet pipe thickly one large circle the size of a tea plate. Brush with egg and sprinkle with almonds. Bake in centre of pre-heated oven for 15 minutes, then reduce heat to (375°F. or Gas Mark 5), for another 25—30 minutes or until choux is dried out and crisp. When cold split horizontally in half and fill with Crème Pâtissière previously flavoured with praline paste and enriched with the butter. Dust heavily with icing sugar.

Note

If preferred you can make individual Paris-Brest.

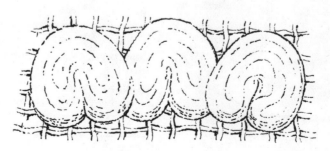

INDEX

ACKNOWLEDGEMENTS

The Author and Publishers would like to thank the following for their help in supplying pictures for this book:

Birds Eye Foods Limited; Brown and Polson Limited; The Cheese Bureau; The Chicken Information Council; Colman's Mustard; The Egg Marketing Board; The Flour Advisory Bureau; Françoise Bernard, Société Astra-Calvé; The French Government Tourist Office; La Favourite Mustard; MacFisheries Limited; The Mushroom Growers Association; The New Zealand Lamb Information Bureau; The Potato Marketing Board; P. R. Visuals Limited; Sopexa, London-French National Organisation for the promotion of French food, wine and agricultural products; Photos O.P.G. Paris; Ulster Bacon; The White Fish Authority.

seine

MUSCADET

CÔTEAUX de TOURAINE

Lo

SANCERRE

QUINC

REUILLY

ANJOU

dordogn

ENTRE
DEUX ME

BORDEAUX

garonne

GAILLA

JURANÇON

ROUSSILLO